Endorsement for Between Preachers

My wife, Alisa, and I were in the first Interim Ministry workshop Jerrie conducted. It was most informative and helpful. This book is an excellent summary of the workshop and thorough guide to getting started in interim ministry, and for churches to understand how it can work positively. There are supplementary resource recommendations inside. Preachers, elders, deacons and other church members can work toward better communication, relationships, transitions, and longer term preacher tenures by using the ideas in this book.
— Roger L. Leonard

I very much endorse your book on leadership training, and the Between Preachers Ministry. I have fond memories of the time you spent with us in a leadership workshop, and the value of your credible information on this much needed ministry. Your insightful knowledge and expertise in the field of leadership training, along with a "hands-on" presentation, has helped us greatly as elders at the Puyallup Church of Christ.
— Ken Wilson, Ph.D., President, Agape Counseling Center

Jerrie Barber encourages his audiences, 'Try not to learn too much.' Jerrie's chronicled work "Between Preachers" takes the many "mustard seeds" he has gained and sows them among those willing to learn. This book will help any reader navigate the mountain of transition with the faith and grace our Lord is seeking for His people."

—Dr. Bryan McAlister - Walnut St. Church of Christ and Freed-Hardeman University-Dickson

Jerrie Barber's wisdom and experience have brought me through the highs and lows of ministry. Every church leader needs Jerrie Barber and now they are able through his new book.
— Andy Walker

Having experienced Jerrie's interim ministry training, having read his writings, having followed him in a local church after one of his interim ministries...I can testify to just how invaluable his ministry and messages are. This book is balanced. It is biblically based and filled with practical wisdom gained from experience.
— Dean Miller, Widowhood Workshop Ministry

Jerrie Barber has relevant, enormous, and rare skills. He understands the difference between theory and theology. He is gifted at translating concepts into action for himself and others. And, his depth of expertise makes what is complex look simple without ever oversimplifying. He is, hands down, the most trusted practitioner I know in doing interim ministry.
— Randy Willingham, D.Min., Director, Harding University Center for Spiritual Leadership

Jerrie Barber is one of those rare people who never stops learning from the best authors and mines his experiences and resources into practical tools that others can use. My conversations with Jerrie are always invigorating and enriching. This book is no different. It is like a conversation with a seasoned practitioner who is deeply convicted about helping churches in transition. He integrates insights from leading experts with his keen awareness of human interactions and congregational life. Churches who use this book during ministry transitions will be equipped against common mistakes and aimed toward best practices. I recommend this book as a tool for healthy calibration when a church is between preachers.

— Dr. Carlus Gupton, Professor of Ministry, Harding School of Theology

Between Preachers

Between Preachers

You Can Grow Through Interim Ministry

JERRIE BARBER

ISBN: 978-0-578-62931-5

Published by Jerrie Barber
jerriebarber.com

Interior Layout: Chad Landman & Joey Sparks
Cover Design: Joey Sparks
Professional Editing: Kathy Jarrell & Vikki Stemler

Dedication

I dedicate this book to Gail Champion Barber, my wife and partner in interim ministry and all of my life.

Gail developed the concept of interim ministry before we heard of the Interim Ministry Network or the term interim ministry.

She enjoys meeting and serving new people and congregations. She and I place membership in the congregations where we serve. She teaches, participates, cooks, entertains, visits, listens, talks, and cooperates in every way.

When we are ready to leave, the usual comments are:

"Jerrie, we're going to miss you."

"We're going to keep Gail."

Gail is a vital part of this ministry and my life.

Appreciation

This ministry would not have been possible without the risk and trust of the congregations who have invited us to work with them. For most, this was the first time they had heard of the term and concept of interim ministry.

I am thankful for their trust and cooperation:

1. Eddyville Church of Christ, Eddyville, Kentucky, May 2007–August 2008
2. Hendersonville Church of Christ, Hendersonville, Tennessee, October 2008–December 2009
3. Collegeside Church of Christ, Cookeville, Tennessee, March 2010–June 2011
4. LaVergne Church of Christ, LaVergne, Tennessee, August 2011–June 2013
5. Maury City Church of Christ, Maury City, Tennessee, September 2013–July 2015
6. Northside Church of Christ, Jeffersonville, Indiana, September 2015–February 2017
7. Shady Acres Church of Christ, Sikeston, Missouri, April 2017–August 2018
8. River Road Church of Christ, Nashville, Tennessee, November 2018–present

Table of Contents

Appendix:

Foreword

I remember well the first time I ever heard Jerrie Barber preach. We did not meet that night. In fact, it would be nearly ten more years before that neat opportunity. I have never been around Jerrie when I didn't learn something. His unique approach and thorough thoughtfulness always leave me thinking, "I want to be like that." I think I've learned more from him about minister/elder relations than any group of people put together. It is not surprising that when I wrote my own book about moving I dedicated it to him. *Between Preachers* is a book you'll treasure.

It is unique. Knowing Jerrie, I was not surprised that it has been very well thought out, is chock full of resources, easy to understand, written in enjoyable style, biblical, sensitive, well organized, and just worthwhile in every way.

If I could be in charge of elderships and responsible for helping them learn to better "shepherd the flock that is among them," *Between Preachers* would be required reading. Any eldership that reads this book and takes it to heart will find some things they do not wish to implement—BUT they will be better as a result of having read it.

While brother Jerrie has written the only book I know of by a member of the church of Christ on interim ministry, the excellent principles in this book could well be used as a book on healthy moving, or healthy leader/minister relations, or a book for every Christian on healthy living! I'd encourage you to purchase one for every elder you know.

— Dale Jenkins (Spring Hill, TN)

Introduction:
Have You Noticed?

Often when a preacher has stayed a long time (5 years or more) and leaves, the next preacher usually stays a short time. And often, he is tormented while he is there being unfavorably compared to the previous preacher.

One helpful approach in many congregations is the services of an intentional interim preacher. An intentional interim is one who is prepared by study and experience in the dynamics of transition and Biblical principles. Leaving Egypt (previous state), wandering through the wilderness with complaining, wishing to make it like it used to be, and eventually entering the promised land where God's people can enjoy another season of growth in carrying out the Great Commission, he understands he is temporary. He signs a contract. He will not consider or be considered as the next preacher of this congregation. He does what he promised.

I've enjoyed preaching since June 18, 1961. I've experienced frustration, helplessness, and seasons of depression while serving two unintentional interims. An unintentional interim is a preacher who begins a work intending to stay a long time. He follows a beloved preacher who's stayed a long time—five or more years. The unintentional interim either doesn't have the knowledge and wisdom to suffer the pain of being unfavorably compared to the previous preacher or doesn't have the hope that he can make a difference. After a short time, he leaves. The congregation also suffers. It would be difficult to adequately grieve the loss of your spouse if you got married the day after the funeral.

My wife and I studied interim ministry with the Interim Ministry Network 1998-1999. I went for a refresher course in March 2007, immediately before starting interim ministry. Gail and I have been working with churches BETWEEN PREACHERS since May 2007. We are working with the eighth congregation now.

An interim preacher provides the congregation with consistent, pointed, and challenging sermons and Bible classes while the congregation is preparing and pursuing the next located long term preacher. People can see a plan.

The interim will lead individuals, small groups, and the whole church in learning experiences to grieve the loss of the previous preacher, along with working on any present conflict, anticipating the next season of growth.

This book describes procedures and results of understanding that wilderness time is not wasted. God didn't make a mistake by not sending the children of Israel into Canaan twelve days after they left Egypt.

Often people ask, "Where did you get the idea for interim ministry?"

Gail and I married August 18, 1964. Soon after we married, we discussed what we would do when we retired. Retirement was not quitting work but changing gears.

I had observed preachers who weren't in full-time works and wanted to continue preaching, hold revivals and workshops. So I said, "We'll hold meetings and workshops. We'll travel, get to know many people, and serve in that way."

Several years later, we were continuing our discussion. Gail said, "When you hold a meeting, you do a good job. But when you preach for a church Sunday through Wednesday, ten years later, what do they remember? Not much. What I'd like to do is to go to a church, work with them six months to a year, then go to another. You could preach and teach classes. I could teach ladies' Bible classes and serve in other ways."

I replied, "That would be great but I don't know how to do it."

Some time later, I was listening to a series of lectures on divorce by Gale Napier, a Christian counselor. He said, "If you get a divorce and think you might want to get married again, you probably ought to wait at least two years or you'll have more people in the bed than you can sleep with."

That rang a bell with me. That's what we do with preachers. A preacher stays with a church ten, twenty, thirty, or more years. He moves, retires, is released, or dies. What most members want the elders to do is have another preacher ready to start. We want to have a going-away party for the old preacher one Sunday and have the next preacher start the next Sunday. Then we're amazed many people don't accept the new preacher because he isn't like the old preacher. One preacher told me he was invited to a potluck where he had tried out. They had invited the top two preachers of all that had tried out. They were to announce the one that had been selected. My friend lost (or won). The other preacher was the pick. My friend said it was an awkward day. No one wanted to talk with him. They didn't know what to say. He didn't know what to say. This is similar to my experiences in being an unintentional interim. When you move to work with a church where they aren't ready for a new preacher, the awkwardness lasts much longer than a Sunday afternoon.

I started telling people this was what I wanted to do when I finished full-time preaching, "If any church will let me, I want to work with a congregation where the preacher has left. I don't want to be the next preacher, but I want to work with them while they are looking for another preacher." I thought we'd come up with a new idea.

Many people encouraged me in this. They began to recount many churches where the new preacher was rejected, not because he wasn't a good man and a good preacher, but because he wasn't like brother John who had just left.

About a year later, I read in Leadership Journal about the Interim Ministry Network. This group was started in 1981. I wrote to the IMN, paid my dues, and began to receive their publications. In 1996, Gail and I attended their conference and were impressed with their insights on the transition process.

In 1998-1999, Gail, John Parker, and I participated in their training. We had five days of classroom work, six months of field work, followed by five more days of class instruction. Interim Ministry Network teaches many skills helpful to any church leader. They rely on Family Systems (Bowen Theory) in viewing how groups behave. The insights I received helped me during the remaining years of full-time ministry at Berry's Chapel in Franklin, Tennessee. My last day there was April 1, 2007.

I look forward to sharing with you what I've learned in reading, training, and especially what I've observed from preaching since 1961 and interim ministry since 2007.

When a preacher stays a long time, usually the church doesn't like the next preacher. I volunteer to be the next preacher they don't like. During the six to eighteen months Gail and I work with them, they have time to grieve their losses and wisely select their next preacher. This book describes how we do it.

The map-chart-summary on the following page summarizes the interim process described in this book.

Let's begin our journey through the wilderness to the promised land.

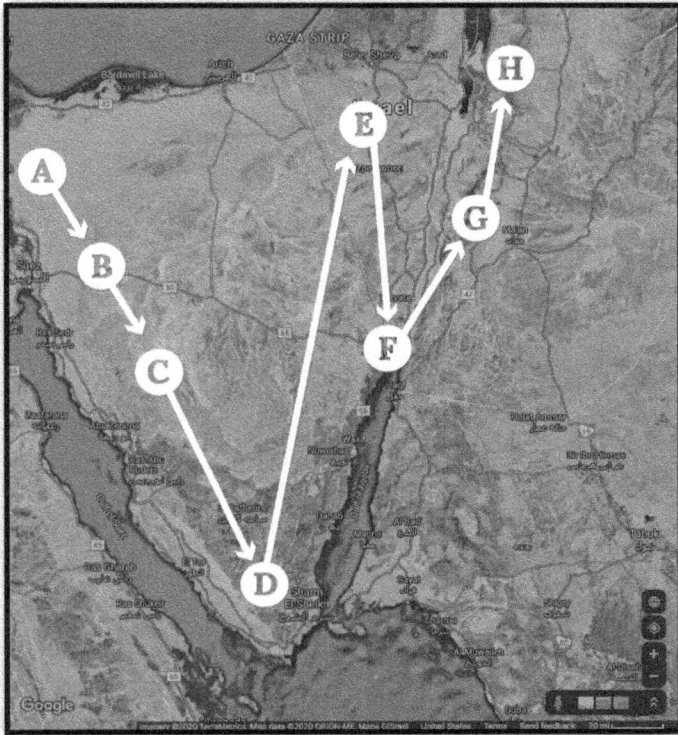

The Journey Between Preachers

A. The preacher leaves. (Chapters 1 & 2)

B. How will this family (church) work through this transition? (Chapters 3-10)

C. Should we use a guide (Interim Minister)? (Chapters 11-15)

D. Begin the interim process. (Chapters 16-23)

E. Learn in the wilderness (interim). (Chapters 24-31)

F. Search for the next preacher. (Chapters 32-41)

G. Finish your interim work. (Chapters 42-43)

H. When you don't need an interim. (Chapter 44)

Chapter 1
How Can We Improve Without Changing?
The Desire of Many in Transition

If we could just get it back the way it used to be.

The Israelites wanted to go back to Egypt where the food was better. Christians in a congregation where there has been conflict, want everyone to come back. "Let's get a new preacher and get it back the way it used to be." "Let's appoint a new elder to replace the one who resigned, died, moved, or left angry."

Why not just announce there'll be no more change and keep things predictable and peaceful?

Without change, you have perpetual babies, freshmen, entry-level jobs, immature Christians, unqualified leaders, or no leaders.

Change IS. Change happens — often without our choice and control. Many times change is from the outside. Transition happens on the inside. I have choices of how I respond to change.

William Bridges was a frustrated, burned-out college professor. He decided to take some time off and decide what he wanted to do with the rest of his life. He became a transition specialist.

He divided a transition into three stages:
1. An ending.
2. A neutral zone.
3. A new beginning.

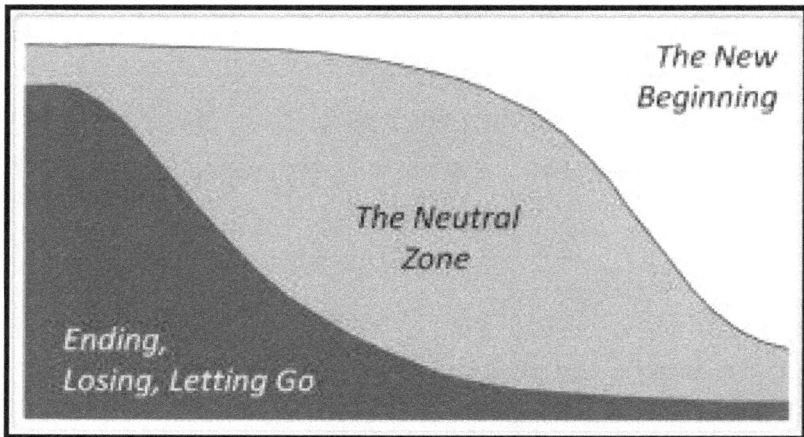

The key to understanding the process is accepting and trying to deal with the neutral zone. During this time one is confused, disoriented, and often loses hope.

Mr. Bridges said trying to make things like they used to be is like taking a handful of leaves in one hand in November and a tube of Elmer's Glue™ in the other. When someone asks,

"What are you doing?", you reply, "I'm gluing leaves back on the tree. I like trees with leaves better."

Here is the hope. Mr. Bridges said you don't have to do much during the neutral zone — during the winter. Just keep from freezing to death. Winter will pass. Spring will come. Things will never be just like they were. But trees will put out leaves. Flowers will bloom. There'll be another growing season.

A good understanding of this process has been helpful to me. Notice the chart. There aren't three neat horizontal stages. They overlap. Some days you will be sad thinking of what you have lost, ecstatic as you think of great things ahead, and depressed because you don't know what to do next.

I've read three books by Bridges:

Transitions: Making Sense of Life's Changes. This is the theory, a good explanation of the process.

Managing Transitions: Making the Most of Change. This is the how-to book. There are suggestions and procedures for leaders or individuals to deal with change to make a better transition.

The Way of Transition: Embracing Life's Most Difficult Moments.
He tells how he dealt with the illness and death of his wife, his
grieving, and eventual remarriage. He describes vividly how
powerful the neutral zone is:

> All the things that I had written about transition – the
> very things that people had said were so helpful to them
> – now felt strangely unreal to me. I wondered, How
> could I ever have tried to pass myself off as an expert on
> transition? I felt now that my words had totally failed to
> match in depth the experience of actually being in
> transition (*The Way of Transition: Embracing Life's Most
> Difficult Moments*, by William Bridges Copyright © 2001
> by William Bridges, page xii).

Part of understanding transition is that it takes time. You can
assign as many women as you can recruit, but it'll still take
about nine months to have a baby. I cannot successfully
command someone else or myself to "Get over it."

The opportunity for the interim minister is to coach and lead
the congregation during this uncertain time. Confusion,
anxiety, and lack of direction are normal for people grieving
over a loss and wondering if there'll be a new beginning.

This process is what I plan to discuss in this book.

Chapter 2

How Long Will it Take?
Why Can't We Just Get On With the Lord's Work?

It was my first day as interim preacher at this congregation. I taught Bible class and preached Sunday morning and Sunday night. We were having a Family Meeting after evening services. After setting rules of discussion, it was time for questions.

A good sister was ready: "Brother Barber, nothing against you, but I don't think we need an interim preacher. We've always just gone out and got another preacher in the past and that's what I think we need to do this time. We need to get on with the Lord's work."

My reply, "With that kind of honesty, there's much hope for this church." This sister was kind to me and was one of my best encouragers. She shared her food and her thoughts. She asked a question many have thought about the interim process.

Why do we have to do a self-study, reflect on our past, dream about the future, think about the kind of preacher we need, devise a thoughtful plan for the search, take the time we need to get to know prospective preachers and encourage them to get to know us, interview, check references, pray for us, pray for the preacher and his family who will come to work with us, pray for the preachers who wanted to come but were eliminated in favor of the one selected, and finally welcome a new preacher a year or two later?

Why go through all this? We've never done it this way before. Why can't we just get on with the Lord's work?

If the alternator goes out on my car, I want it fixed. I take it to the mechanic. He removes the old, installs the new, and my car is fixed. Many want to "fix" the church like they fix their automobile.

However, let's suppose there are two couples in their fifties. A man in one couple and woman in the other dies within a few months of each other. It might be great for the surviving spouses to marry each other.

Conventional wisdom says they need to wait a few months after the funeral. People aren't machines. The emotional process of grief takes time. One relationship needs to have some closure before a new one begins for the new one to be most effective.

Often when people are fondly recalling their former preacher – repeating something he said, or telling how he did something

— someone will say, "They have preacher-itis." Certainly Paul addressed harmful allegiance to men causing division in the church at Corinth (1 Corinthians 1:1-15). It isn't right to follow a human instead of Jesus. It isn't right to cause division in the church because of personalities.

But, it may be that some people are dealing with the loss of a preacher, a brother in Christ, and a friend, in a normal way.

Does a woman who is depressed, angry, disoriented, sad, and crying have "husband-itis" after her companion of twenty or more years is buried?

Did Job's wife have "oxen-itis," "donkey-itis," "sheep-itis," "camel-itis," and "child-itis" when she said to her sick husband, "Do you still hold fast to your integrity? Curse God and die!" (Job 2:9, NKJV)? Years ago, I was critical of Mrs. Job for this statement. But I've never attended the funeral for all my children in one day while going from being one of the richest persons in my community and losing every investment and the health of my companion in a short time.

Did Mary and Martha have "brother-itis" when they individually said to Jesus when he came to visit, "Lord, if You had been here, my brother would not have died" (John 11:21, 32)?

The normal human reaction to loss is grief.

To deny people the right to work through their feelings of sadness, anger, fear, and jealousy or their feelings of joy, guilt, and frustration (depending on whether the person is one who wanted the preacher to go or stay) is to create an atmosphere to act out in an unhealthy way what could be talked out in a beneficial exchange. Perhaps listening and asking questions to allow more talking would be more helpful than being critical and assigning a negative label to the person talking about the recently departed preacher.

This is one of the benefits of interim ministry. A trained interim sees complimentary comments about the previous preacher as a normal part of the transition process and isn't threatened. The interim preacher doesn't come to replace the previous preacher. He's working in the congregation in the in-between times. Part of the service of an interim is to "be there" to allow time for grief and adjustment after a long ministry or during a time of conflict.

Several years ago I taught a class on grief, discussing various stages and how people progressed at different speeds. A good deacon came after class and said, "I take three days to grieve after a death and get over it."

A few years later his wife developed cancer and died. He remembered his statement in class. He said it took longer than three days!

Was Jesus "doing the Lord's work" when He wept at Lazarus' death?

Are we "doing the Lord's work" when we "weep with those who weep" (Romans 12:15)?

Chapter 3
What (Who) Is the Problem?
Can We Fix It Quickly?

When I come into a group with conflict, I find people are struggling and want quick relief. To get that, we have to believe the problem is easy to understand and will be easy to fix.

When you see a serious problem in your group (family, church, business, or softball team), how do you proceed? In the Dale Carnegie class, I learned four problem-solving questions that have helped in several situations:

1. What is the problem?
2. What are the causes of the problem?
3. What are possible solutions?
4. What is the best possible solution?

One way to try to get it fixed, is to change the first question from "What is the problem?" to "Who is the problem?". If we can find the person causing the problem, and convert or eliminate him or her, we've solved the problem. This is the starting point of "death wishes for leaders." Have you heard the statement, "I'll tell you what it's gonna take to get this church (business, club) straightened out — a few good funerals!"?

If that's true, do you want to see the church get straightened out? How soon? Whom do you want to see die in the next few weeks?

Is there a better approach to see the church grow than wishing people dead?

It's my understanding from decades of observation and some Bible study that if a problem is chronic (more than a few weeks old), there's more than one person "causing" the problem. "Fixing" one person by changing or eliminating him or her will only change where the problem presents itself.

The second proposed way to get quick relief from a problem is to preach a sermon on forgiveness and tell everyone to immediately forgive everyone of everything–during the invitation song as we stand and sing. That should cure all ills.

Yet, I've noticed the person who needs to be "fixed" fails to get the message. Often people who've been abused for years come forward to be restored and to forgive. But the problem remains.

That solution also disregards Jesus' instruction in Luke 17:3, "Take heed to yourselves. If your brother sins against you, rebuke him; and if he repents, forgive him." That may take longer than the fourth verse of the invitation song.

In contrast to these two quick solutions to complicated issues, I've found it helpful to have a model of how groups work.

The basic principle I've learned from Family Systems is to "mind my own business."

- Listen before I talk.
- Learn before I teach.
- Examine myself before I blame others.

We'll look at five basic principles of Family Systems to help us ponder what we can do, individually, to help in times of anxiety.

Chapter 4

Principle 1 of Family Systems:
The Identified Patient: What's Wrong With Him (Us)?

Often a family will name one of its members as the "black sheep." A church will pick a person or a group in the congregation and label him or them as "the problem." If we could only fix "the problem" or if we could convert the "black sheep," the family or church would be okay.

The concept of family systems: if a situation is chronic – if the symptoms are recurring or of long duration – it's not the "fault" of one person. It is because the family "likes it that way." The family prefers the way it is rather than being willing to endure the pain and effort it would take to change it.

Edwin Friedman, in the first chapter of his book, *Generation to Generation* (© 1985 The Guilford Press), explained the concept of the identified patient. The family member with the obvious symptom is not to be seen as the "sick one" but as the one in whom the family's stress or pathology has surfaced. Physicians don't assume the part of a human organism in pain, or failing to act properly, is necessarily the cause of its own distress. Problems in any organ may relate to excessive over functioning, under functioning, or dis-functioning of another. By keeping the focus on one of its members, the family, personal or congregational, can deny the very issues that contributed to making one of its members symptomatic, even if it ultimately harms the entire family.

A doctor doesn't suggest someone who comes to him with yellow skin call the Avon lady. He'll probably start by looking at the liver. Although the skin is yellow, it didn't begin in the skin.

My father had bypass surgery in 1981. In February 1998, he was having pains in his jaw. He asked my wife, "Gail, do you think the pain in my jaw could have anything to do with my heart?". She assured him that was a distinct possibility. He called his doctor on Monday. Tuesday he had an angiogram. Wednesday he had his second bypass surgery. He had a pain in his jaw. He didn't need to see a dentist. It was heart disease.

Often when I'm consulting with congregations, the identified patient is "leadership." Brothers tell me, "Our problem is a lack of effective leadership." I ask how long this has been an issue. Usually, it's been an issue for years. It's my observation a church has the leaders it wants. It has leaders it's trained, prayed for, encouraged, and tolerated. It's too late to be concerned about the quality of leadership two weeks before time to appoint shepherds or deacons. A series of sermons from 1 Timothy 3 and Titus 1 won't make up for years of neglect in making disciples of Jesus.

Paul describes how the body is connected and how members affect each other in 1 Corinthians 12:26, "And if one member suffers, all the members suffer with it; or if one member is honored, all the members rejoice with it." We rarely have an individual problem of long duration. It's a family problem. If we fail to recognize this, we may fix "the problem" (identified patient) but if the family doesn't change, the symptoms will resurface in the same patient or another because forces that contributed to "the problem" are still there.

Do you know of a congregation that's fired most of its preachers? Who selects preachers? Who interacts with preachers, encourages preachers, and discourages preachers? Are they consistently choosing bad preachers? Who did that? Do they select good preachers and good preachers become bad after they arrive? Will you solve the problem by choosing another bad preacher or a good preacher who will be micro-managed or ignored and criticized until he leaves?

We need to ask the same questions about all leadership. Who selects leaders? Who encourages elders and deacons in their work? Does the group approve or say nothing when unqualified men are considered? Do many in the congregation begin to criticize and question motives of anyone appointed to leadership? How long has it been since many people or the group expressed sincere, specific, and sustained appreciation to the leaders, individually and as a group?

I heard Ira North say, "We put a man in an ice house and cuss him out for not sweating."

If a church has a leadership deficiency, I wonder, "Why do they like it that way?"

In his book, *Healthy Congregations* (Copyright © 1996 The Alban Institute, Inc.), Peter Steinke gives two quotes about this principle:

- It is more important to know what sort of patient has the disease than what sort of disease the patient has.
  — Sir William Osler (page 23).
- The healthy society, like the healthy body, is not the one that has taken the most medicine. It is the one in which the internal health building force is in the best shape.
  — Peter Senge (page 101).

When "the problem" has been in a church, family, business, or softball team for years, a good question for the group would be, "I wonder why we like it that way and would we be willing to endure the pain to change it (us)?".

Chapter 5

Principle 2 of Family Systems:
Homeostasis (Balance): How Can We Improve and Stay the Same (Not Change)?

———————

"This is the worst thing that ever happened. We've got to do something to fix it. I'm tired of all this turmoil. It's time for things to get back to normal."

People will get anxious when things get worse in their life. People will get anxious when things in their life get significantly better because that also is out of their comfort zone.

I knew a man who had been successful in his business for many years. However, conditions changed and it looked like he might face bankruptcy. He became cranky and depressed.

He held on to his business and worked out of the crisis. After a few years when he filled out his financial statement, his net worth exceeded one million dollars! How do you think he felt? Do you think he was happy and celebrated? He wasn't, and he didn't. He became cranky and depressed. Both conditions were out of his comfort zone. A thermostat keeps the temperature in a room in a comfortable range, making adjustments when it gets too hot or too cold. People seem to have a corrective command to keep conditions in their lives from getting too bad or too good.

Edwin Friedman in *Generation to Generation* explains homeostasis as "the tendency of any set of relationships to strive perpetually, in self-corrective ways, to preserve the organizing principles of its existence." He asks the question, "Why has the symptom surfaced now? This is not a static concept, but a dynamic one, as when a thermostat controls the temperature balance, not at a fixed point, but within a range" (page 23, © 1985 The Guilford Press).

In a church, family, business, or softball team, the focus on the identified patient (black sheep) and resistance from those who are peacekeepers instead of peacemakers explain why the group will tolerate and adapt to trouble-making complainers and incompetent leaders and members. On the other hand, the person who encourages personal responsibility, growth, and confronting the long-term problems, will be ignored, if not let go.

Peter Steinke comments:

"Actually religious institutions are the worst offenders at encouraging immaturity and irresponsibility. In church after church, some member is passively-aggressively holding the whole system hostage, and no one wants to fire him or force her to leave because it wouldn't be 'the Christian thing to do.' It has nothing to do with Christianity. Synagogues also tolerate abusers because it wouldn't be the Christian thing to do" (*How Your Church Family Works*, Copyright © 1993 The Alban Institute, Inc., page 59).

This sabotage to keep homeostasis is a major obstacle in any system (family, business, church, or softball team).

Friedman adds,

"The same qualities that allow for 'familiness' (that is, stability) in the first place are precisely what hinder change (that is, less stability) when the family system is too fixed" (*Generation to Generation*, page 25).

Paul was not only concerned with the man committing fornication in Corinth but also with the church who "liked it that way."

It is actually reported that there is sexual immorality among you, and such sexual immorality as is not even named among the Gentiles—that a man has his father's wife! And you are puffed up, and have not rather mourned, that he who has done this deed might be taken away from among you. Your glorying is not good. Do you not know that a little leaven leavens the whole lump? (1 Corinthians 5:1, 2, 6).

Often in talking with people in groups (families, churches, businesses, or softball teams) an individual will describe and deplore the "identified patient," the person "causing the problem." I ask, "Why do you like it that way?". If a condition is chronic, the group likes it the way it is more than they desire what it would take to change it. When individuals see how they are supporting the condition, they can regain hope that things can be different.

Chapter 6
Principle 3 of Family Systems
Differentiation: How Can We Be Connected — But Not Stuck?

When I am criticized, am I devastated? Do I have difficulty taking a position — stating where I stand — and, if necessary, being in the minority rather than sacrificing my convictions? If the answer is "Yes" to one or both questions, growing in differentiation can improve my leadership. Jesus was the Master of knowing who He was, what He believed, and doing what He needed to do, regardless of consequences.

Edwin Friedman describes this leadership strength as

> the capacity of a family member to define his or her own life's goals and values apart from surrounding togetherness pressures, to say "I" when others are demanding "you" and "we." It includes the capacity to maintain a (relatively) nonanxious presence in the midst of anxious systems, to take maximum responsibility for one's own destiny and emotional being. It can be measured somewhat by the breadth of one's repertoire of responses when confronted with crisis. The concept should not be confused with autonomy or narcissism, however. Differentiation means the capacity to be an "I" while remaining connected

(*Generation to Generation*, page 27, © 1985 The Guilford Press).

Peter Steinke quoted Murray Bowen, the father of family system thinking, in his book, *How Your Church Family Works*:

> "A 'differentiated self' is one who can maintain emotional objectivity, while in the midst of an emotional system in turmoil, yet at the same time actively relate to key people in the system" (page 69, Copyright © 1993 The Alban Institute, Inc.).

This attribute will help me deal with criticism. If I'm in despair when someone points out what he believes is a weakness in me, I'm stuck with his evaluation. There are possibilities when I receive criticism: the criticism is true, partially true, or untrue. If the assessment is valid and I can correct the deficiency, I've learned of an opportunity for growth. If I can't correct the deficiency, I have the challenge to learn contentment with something I can't change. If the accusation isn't true, I don't want to give the misinformed person power over me.

Peter Steinke presented a helpful way to look at criticism:

> By far the most difficult form of pursuit behavior to recognize is criticism. How can those who act adversarially be said to be in pursuit? We feel alienated, not close. But criticism is characterized by overfocus. The "stinger" and

the "stung" are emotionally connected. Whenever a gnawing critic gets inside our brain cells and we can't expunge him, we are connected, even if negatively. Whenever someone gets under our skin, we are infected with anxiety. If we are reactive to a pursuer, the pursuit behavior achieves its goal: connection. Strange as it sounds, the critic wants to be close. After all, if we can't be close through play, ecstasy, touch, and nurture, our only option to accomplish closeness is through angry outbursts, specious charges, or harsh accusations. People feel close to us when they know we are thinking about them. What we think is not as important as that we are thinking about them. We play into the hands of criticizers when we react to their invasion rather than define ourselves to it (*How Your Church Family Works*, pages 88, 89).

If that's true, a critic values me. When I am differentiated, often I can establish, reestablish, or strengthen a relationship with the critic and be his friend and servant.

My hero and model of this quality of differentiation is Joshua. Listen to his farewell speech to Israel:

Now therefore, fear the Lord, serve Him in sincerity and in truth, and put away the gods which your fathers served on the other side of the River and in Egypt. Serve the Lord! And if it seems evil to you to serve the Lord, choose for yourselves this day whom you will serve, whether the gods which your fathers served that were on the other side of the River, or the gods of the Amorites, in whose land you dwell. But as for me and my house, we will serve the Lord (Joshua 24:14, 15).

1. He told them what was right.
2. He recognized he could not and should not control them. They were responsible for their choices. He acknowledged that and enumerated alternatives they may not have considered.
3. He defined himself. Although they had many choices, he wasn't taking a vote on how he should act. He told them where he stood.

When a leader is growing in this quality, he feels no need to take sides in a conflict. He can understand what people are saying on different sides of the issue. He's aware of strengths and weaknesses of people involved. He talks when it's helpful and refrains from comments when what he might say wouldn't help solve the problem.

Chapter 7

Principle 4 of Family Systems:
Extended Family Field: Were (Are) My Relatives Human?

How much of your leadership is influenced by your family? How could learning more about your family improve your effectiveness as a leader?

Although people aren't predetermined to follow their parents, they may be predisposed because of their environment and training. A leader may improve his/her leadership by learning more about his/her extended family.

The phrase, "extended family field," refers to our family of origin, (parents, brothers, sisters) plus our other relatives (grandparents, aunts, uncles, cousins, etc.). Edwin Friedman describes the differences in outlook of the individual model of groups and the family systems model:

> The thinking that surrounds the individual model tends to see the extended family field almost exclusively as the source of difficulties or pathology. The family becomes something to learn to deal with so that it won't get you. The model tends to focus on what is sick or weak in the family, what to avoid or keep at a distance. It therefore encourages

individuals with problems to see their family of origin only as a source of their weakness and not as also a source of their strengths. The family systems model enables individuals to seek relationships with their family of origin; the problem with parents, after all, is that they had parents (*Generation to Generation*, page 35).

This approach recognizes most families and most human beings making up those families have both good and bad characteristics. This approach permits us to recognize both – to find and incorporate the strengths in the system.

It's my observation that many people see their family members as more than or less than human. Those who see them as more than human (angels) do not recognize they had faults. "My father would never have done anything wrong. My parents were perfect. I never remember a mistake they made." They were more than human.

Others had painful experiences in their family. "My mother was a devil. She was evil through and through." Those who see their family members as less than human (demons) want to separate from them and never have contact with them.

More than likely, our relatives were human. They had strengths and weaknesses. God has given us freedom of choice to learn from and imitate the good and learn from and reject what is less than best.

We have choices of following the strengths or weaknesses of our family. Men and women didn't get their names in Hebrews 11 because of perfection but because of strengths God chose to emphasize and exemplify. How did God want us to remember the heroes of faith in this great chapter of the Bible?

- Will we follow Noah's faith and obedience or his drunkenness? v. 7
- God recorded Abraham's faith and obedience in Hebrews 11, not his lying, and laughing. vv. 8-10, 17-19
- Moses makes it into the Hall of Faith because of his courageous, wise choices, not his murder. vv. 24-27
- Rahab is listed for her respect for God, not for her prostitution and lying. v. 31
- Samson is known for his sacrificial dedication at the end of his life, not his many sins mentioned in Judges. v. 32
- David is known as a man after God's own heart, for his repentance and continual search for God, not for his adultery and murder. v. 32

Individuals in families tend to do what that family has always done.

"That's the way the Jones family is — we've always had trouble with our temper."

> The Lord is longsuffering and abundant in mercy, forgiving iniquity and transgression; but He by no means clears the guilty, visiting the iniquity of the fathers on the children to the third and fourth generation (Numbers 14:18).

However, if we get to know our families better (for two or more generations back), we may be able to see strengths and imitate them, and release weaknesses and not do them just because "that's the way we've always done it." This long-range objective is a goal of family systems.

Getting to know my family better and why they do the things they do has freed me to decide whether I want to do things the way we've always done it, rebel and reverse everything, or consider the options and do what I think best in each circumstance. I have used questions I read in *Family Ties that Bind*, by Ronald W. Richardson to discuss our family rules—conscious and unconscious—with members of my family. *See Appendix: Questions to Learn More About Your Family.*

It's been helpful to me to see that congregations also form a family system. The more I understand the congregation as a family system, I can be freer to do what God teaches me is best

— not just repeat something because "that's the way we've always done it" or reject it because "that's the way we've always done it."

Chapter 8
Principle 5 of Family Systems:
Emotional Triangle: How Can I Keep From Getting Caught in the Middle?

One frustrating situation in leadership is getting caught in the middle of a conflict. People involved in a dispute have expected me to be the judge or at least "straighten out" the other person. Many elders, preachers, parents, and other human beings find themselves in this predicament.

Edwin Friedman describes this dilemma:

An emotional triangle is formed by any three persons or issues...

> The basic law of emotional triangles is that when any two parts of a system become uncomfortable with one another, they will "triangle in" or focus upon a third person, or issue, as a way of stabilizing their own relationship with one another. A person may be said to be "triangled" if he or she gets caught in the middle as the focus of such an unresolved issue. When individuals try to change the relationship of two others (two people, or a person and his or her symptom or belief), they "triangle" themselves into that relationship (and often stabilize the very situation they

are trying to change) (*Generation to Generation: family process in church and synagogue*, pages 35, 36, © 1985 The Guilford Press).

He continues by listing and explaining the seven laws of an emotional triangle. I'm only giving the list here. He expands on each of these in his book. (This is one of the most helpful books I've read [four times], devoured, discussed. Two of the four times I read it, were in staff meetings. We took twenty-two months to read it the first time and seventeen months the second time, reading about three or four pages a week.)

1. The relationship of any two members of an emotional triangle is kept in balance by the way a third party relates to each of them or to their relationship.

2. If one is the third party in an emotional triangle it is generally not possible to bring change (for more than a week) to the relationship of the other two parts by trying to change their relationships directly.

3. Attempts to change the relationship of the other two sides of an emotional triangle not only are generally ineffective, but also, homeostatic forces often convert these efforts to their opposite intent.

4. To the extent a third party to an emotional triangle tries unsuccessfully to change the relationship of the other two, the more likely it is that the third party will wind up with the stress of the other two.

5. The various triangles in an emotional system interlock so that efforts to bring change to any one of them is often resisted by homeostatic forces in the others or in the system itself.

6. One side of an emotional triangle tends to be more conflicted than the others.

7. We can only change a relationship to which we belong (*Generation to Generation*, pages 35-39).

Peter Steinke expands on this concept in his book, *Healthy Congregations: a systems approach*, Copyright © 1996 The Alban Institute, Inc.):

"When elephants fight," a Swahili proverb states, "it's the grass that gets crushed." Triangulation is a natural way of handling anxiety. If anxiety in one relationship is not resolved, it will be played out in another relationship. A person feels relief from tension when anxiety is shifted to a third party, yet the anxiety in the original relationship is unchanged. It has merely relocated.

You know a triangle exists when you experience the following:
- The reactivity being expressed toward you is excessive, strong, and far beyond what might be normal.
- Someone is over-focused on you.
- You look for a sympathetic third person who will share your irritation with an adversary.
- You turn to a second party to talk about a third party.
- You become allied with a friend against your friend's opponent.
- You need to rescue, care for your friend when he or she is anxious.
- You pin your anxiety on someone to relieve tension that belongs to another relationship (page 62).

God has given instructions and warnings about this in the Bible:

The first one to plead his cause seems right, Until his neighbor comes and examines him (Proverbs 18:17).

You shall not go about as a talebearer among your people; nor shall you take a stand against the life of your neighbor: I am the Lord (Leviticus 19:16).

Jesus taught "straight talk" on the part of everyone in a conflicted relationship.

Therefore if you bring your gift to the altar, and there remember that your brother has something against you, leave your gift there before the altar, and go your way. First be reconciled to your brother, and then come and offer your gift (Matthew 5:23, 24).

Moreover if your brother sins against you, go and tell him his fault between you and him alone. If he hears you, you have gained your brother. But if he will not hear, take with you one or two more, that 'by the mouth of two or three witnesses every word may be established.' And if he refuses to hear them, tell it to the church. But if he refuses even to hear the church, let him be to you like a heathen and a tax collector (Matthew 18:15-17).

The following paragraphs are from the *Full-Time Minister Relationships and Responsibilities*, Anytown Church, a congregation where I served as an interim, incorporated in the preacher's working agreement:

Conflict Resolution

In any case of conflict at all times, it is expected that the minister practice guidelines Jesus gave in Matthew 18:15-17.

The minister will be expected to refer members that bring a complaint concerning one elder or the eldership in general to Matthew 18 and encourage them to bring the concern to the elder if it involves one, or to the eldership if it involves the entire eldership.

By the same token, if an elder or the eldership has a complaint brought to them concerning the minister, the same action will be taken. The eldership will not entertain complaints unless the member practices Biblical conflict resolution first.

What if we added another paragraph as a family rule at Anytown Church?:

If any member has a complaint brought to them concerning any other Christian in this congregation, it is expected that the Christian practice guidelines Jesus gave in Matthew 18:15-17. No member will entertain complaints against another brother or sister unless the one making the criticism practices Biblical conflict resolution first including talking to the person alone, then talking again with one or two other people present to help restore the good, loving, and kind relationship.

Following His teaching would eliminate the harmful triangle. The most common response I hear is, "I'm not comfortable doing this." I need to remember that crucifixion is uncomfortable. A follower of Jesus volunteers to carry a cross daily (Luke 9:23).

Chapter 9
I Don't Like It This Way!
But I Like It the Way It Is Better than What It Would Take to Change It

---

The time of transition is painful for many people. A favorite preacher has left. The elders have made unwise choices — or no choices. People are gossiping and saying unkind, inflammatory things. The contribution and attendance are often down. In more serious cases, many have left for other congregations, started a new congregation, or quit public worship altogether.

People want others to change so they can be happy again. Somebody should talk to the elders to tell them to do their work properly. Someone needs to visit the people who left and get them back. Somebody must stop the loose tongues!

"I thought we had a perfect church. I don't know if I'll ever be happy again."

"Why doesn't everyone do what's right?"

"Is there anything I can do when everyone else is making mistakes?"

1. Could I, should I talk with the elders about my concerns? Will I do that with compassion realizing they aren't feeling great in the midst of turmoil in a group they're leading?

2. As an elder, can I listen kindly and with an interest in gaining more wisdom? Is it possible that an ordinary member who "doesn't know all the elders know" can still have something to say and to teach me? Is this Christian who's speaking to me one that I should esteem better than myself (Philippians 2:3)?

3. Do I have a responsibility to show concern for people who are weak, discouraged, or in sin? Am I a spiritual person (Galatians 6:1)?

4. Have I encouraged gossiping people by listening to them, reading their emails and Facebook posts, and saying nothing to them about delivering mail to the right address (Matthew 18:15-17; Proverbs 26:20)?

The apostle Paul is a good example of one who had horrible conditions but kept his faith and joy and remained contented. When he wrote to the Philippians, he was in a dirty, stinking, Roman jail.

John McRay wrote in *Christian History*:

Roman imprisonment was preceded by being stripped naked and then flogged — a humiliating, painful, and bloody ordeal. The bleeding wounds went untreated as prisoners sat in painful leg or wrist chains. Mutilated, bloodstained clothing was not replaced, even in the cold of winter.

Most cells were dark, especially the inner cells of a prison, like the one Paul and Silas inhabited in Philippi. Unbearable cold, lack of water, cramped quarters, and sickening stench from few toilets made sleeping difficult and waking hours miserable. Because of the miserable conditions, many prisoners begged for a speedy death. Others simply committed suicide.

In settings like this, Paul wrote encouraging, even joyful, letters and continued to speak of Jesus (Elesha Coffman, Christian History Connection (6-1-02), from *Christian History* (issue 47); www.preachingtoday.com).

How Paul Responded to Bad Circumstances which Were Not His Fault

1. He was in jail. He used it as an opportunity to evangelize and encourage (Philippians 1:12-14; Philippians 4:22).
2. Some preachers with unchristian attitudes were trying to make his deplorable conditions harder (Philippians 1:15, 16). He chose to rejoice because they were preaching Christ, even though they were insincere

(Philippians 1:16, 17). He selected rejoicing both for the present and the future.

3. He chose contentment. He didn't like it the way it was, but he learned to be content instead of being upset over something he couldn't change (Philippians 4:11, 12).

When a condition in a group — family, church, business, or softball team — is chronic, and a person is disturbed and critical, it's because he likes it the way it is better than doing what it would take to change it.

1. Many refuse or neglect to try to change it because it would be painful and difficult. They don't want to work that hard and suffer that much.
2. When some realize they can't change the situation, they don't want to get an advanced degree in contentment (Paul said he learned it). They don't want to work that hard and suffer that much.
3. So — they suffer in lethargy, discontent, and criticism. There's no escape to suffering (Job 14:1). We get to decide where we'll invest our suffering.

These are some of the opportunities of an interim minister to coach all to be more like Jesus during difficult times.

Chapter 10
Is There Any Hope for This Church?
Should We Trash This One and Start Over?

People are afraid to talk to anyone. Some people they thought were their best friends have left and labeled those who have stayed as "liberal," "radical conservatives," or "without conviction to stand for the truth." "We thought we could trust them. There may be some like those who haven't left. Let's go home. I don't trust anyone. I thought we had the best church in the world." When the congregation has a potluck, food often runs out. People are withholding their conversations, their love, and their green beans. They come late and leave early.

What does an interim preacher say to a church like this in transition? Here's what I say, "This is the day the Lord has made; We will rejoice and be glad in it" (Psalm 118:24).

I follow with several questions:

Do you believe God loves His church? We know He does because He gave the blood of His loving and cooperative Son to buy it (Acts 20:28). His church is valuable to Him. He has a lot invested in it.

Do you believe God loves this congregation? It isn't too bad for Him to love. I enjoy studying 1 Corinthians with a troubled church. This congregation was divided and had arrogant, prideful people in it. A man in Corinth was living with his father's wife, and the rest of the church liked it that way. Brethren were taking each other to court rather than using the principles Jesus taught to settle disputes. They had marriage problems. Idolatry was still a stumbling block with some members. Worship had become a time of separation rather than unity. Some were getting drunk during worship. Spiritual gifts provided the opportunity for believers to continue the apostles' arguments of "who's the greatest in the kingdom." Corinth Church had severe doctrinal problems. There were some who denied a cardinal part of the gospel: resurrection.

When I finish this study, I ask, "Had you rather be a member of this congregation in Anytown, U.S.A. or Corinth?" I haven't had anyone choose Corinth yet.

Notice how Paul addressed this church:

> "To the church of God which is at Corinth, to those who are sanctified in Christ Jesus, called to be saints, with all who in every place call on the name of Jesus Christ our Lord, both theirs and ours" (1 Corinthians 1:2).

It seems the Holy Spirit and Paul have a high regard for what God and His word is able to do with and for sinful people. I've observed many cut and run three weeks, or three months, after the explosion. They think this congregation is hopeless. Paul thought Corinth still had good people and was worth loving and teaching.

Do you believe you can serve God in this congregation? Often people are still trying to decide if they can worship here. "I don't know if I can worship with these elders, those members who gossip, because they let the last preacher go, or because they kept the last preacher too long."

Many choose to go to another congregation or start another church because of sin and shortcomings they see in "the others."

Often people ask me about starting another church. My answer: "To have scriptural encouragement for planting another congregation for a reason other than evangelism, the church you're leaving should be meaner than Corinth and deader than Sardis." Corinth had committed nearly every sin available. I know Sardis was dead because Jesus said it was dead (Revelation 3:1).

Paul chose not to recommend to the saints in Corinth to leave the unfaithful there and start the Faithful Corinth Church. I can't read that anywhere in the book.

Jesus through John wrote to Christians in Sardis,

> You have a few names even in Sardis who have not defiled their garments; and they shall walk with Me in white, for they are worthy (Revelation 3:4).

Neither Jesus nor John recommended the faithful few to leave Dead Sardis Church and start Lively Sardis Church. You and I can be lively Christians in a dead church. How do I know? The Bible tells me so!

Is your church meaner than Corinth or deader than Sardis? No? Then don't start another because you're mad.

Do you believe God will give us wisdom? He promises He will. James, the Lord's brother, told us to pray for wisdom when we need it (James 1:5). The wise man of the Old Testament instructed us to work for wisdom like we work for money and search for it as if we were searching for buried treasure (Proverbs 2:1-5).

What's the big question — Who's in charge of the universe?

If God is God, we have hope, and our faith must be in Him (Hebrews 11:6). If our faith is in people, I understand hopelessness. We can survive and thrive during this time of transition. I like the sentiment I read: "To love the ideal church is easy. To love the real church is difficult." I've never worked with or heard of a church as bad as Corinth or some of the seven congregations in Asia (Revelation 1-3). God loved them enough to send messages of rebuke, correction, and hope.

We can learn from His messages to them and grow during trying times.

Chapter 11
It's Not the Work of the Interim Preacher to Make a Good Transition:
Interim Ministry Isn't Fill-In Preaching

"Jerrie, our elders need fixing. Our deacons don't deak. You need to get members who left to come back. People need to give more. I'm not giving because of what the elders did. What are you going to do to deal with all these problems?"

Not much.

Quite a bit — if what I teach and preach is true and practiced.

Edwin Friedman says one of the greatest mistakes of GOOD leaders is over-functioning. Helicopter parents rarely produce responsible adults.

The work of the interim minister is to help the congregation grow — navigate through a good transition during this time of change from one preacher to another.

Interim ministry is not fill-in preaching. Fill-in preaching is showing up at appointed times and speaking. And good preaching can do much good. But interim ministry calls for more. It's an opportunity to help people think about what's happened and learn from it. I do this from the pulpit, in smaller classes and groups, and in individual conversations.

Different circumstances may call for an interim:

1. The preacher resigned.
2. The preacher died.
3. The preacher was fired.
4. The preacher retired.
5. The preacher stayed for a long time.
6. The last several preachers stayed a short time and left unhappy.
7. The church is in conflict.
8. The church is at peace — so much peace for so long it's about to die. There's a lot of peace in a cemetery.
9. The church is at peace. The last preacher stayed a long time, did a good job, left because he chose to go and believes he made a good decision. People miss him because he was a good preacher, a good servant, and a true friend. No one will ever be able to replace him.
10. The church needs to grieve his absence to get ready to consider who will be the next preacher. It doesn't seem wise to marry a week after burying one's spouse.

And if you're looking for the one you just buried, that person is in the cemetery.

Each of these circumstances requires thoughtful consideration.

In my early ministry, the only method of conflict resolution I knew was to talk with the people involved. I found if I talked to one first, I always talked with the one who was right. I knew he was because he told me he was right and the other person was wrong.

My next step was to get the "wrong one" to come in to talk. The one who was right and I would get the wrong one to repent, and everyone would be happy. They would send me a thank you note and Christmas cards every year.

I've never received my first card from one of those peace conferences. I didn't know and practice Proverbs 18:17:

> The first one to plead his cause seems right, Until his neighbor comes and examines him.

My responsibilities and opportunities are to teach, coach, and encourage people in conflict to follow Jesus and His teaching. If I try to do the work for others, it probably won't work. And if it did, the people failed to exercise their responsibility to follow the Lord's way of repairing broken relationships. If I did their work, they didn't grow from a lack of exercise.

I can't grieve for another.

I can't find the way out of lostness for another.

I can't express and find relief from anger and despair for another.

I may be able to help someone find a better way through the wilderness between the Red Sea and the Promised Land.

My goal is to help, not replace, Christians who are finding their way to a new beginning.

In chapters that follow, I'll relate specifics about what I do as a guide on this adventure.

Chapter 12
Interim Minister Working Agreement:
Good Relationships Begin with Clear Understanding and Mutual Agreements

---

"I didn't know I was supposed to do that."

"You said you were going to do it."

"You agreed to pay me ninety days after we announced I was leaving."

"We don't remember that."

"Check your notes."

"It's not in our minutes."

"Some said they don't like the length of your sermons; a lot of people are upset."

"Who are they?"

"We can't tell you. That information is confidential."

How do you settle these disagreements?

You don't. If no one made an effort and took the time to write agreements, make copies for all parties, and keep them safe for future reference, you won't solve these disputes to everyone's satisfaction.

The only person who doesn't need written agreements is the person who'll never die and who'll never forget anything. If he isn't writing his agreements, he needs to be dealing with people who'll never die and will never forget anything.

It took me ten years and much pain to learn to make agreements of expectations and record those in a working agreement.

Before writing a working agreement, all parties need to have several hours of getting acquainted. I want to hear why the church wants an interim preacher.

- What are their expectations?
- What is their understanding of what I'll do and how long I'll be there?
- What is the difference in an interim minister and a fill-in preacher? What is our understanding of transition?
- Who will be involved in it? How much does each person want to grow or do we just want to get everyone else straightened out?
- What are tasks and groups that need to be included in the transition process?

- How much interaction will there be between the elders and interim preacher?

The working agreement is an official statement of understandings we have reached during our discussions.

Items in Job Working Agreement
1. Job description.
2. Preaching.
3. Teaching.
4. Staff meetings.
5. Organizing transition projects and people.
6. Relationship with elders and staff.
7. Meetings.
8. Communication.
9. Evaluation.
10. Criticism guidelines.
11. Contract.
12. Salary, other benefits.
13. Moving.
14. Time away from the congregation.
15. Study at home and building.
16. Length of work together.
17. 90-day notice of termination.
18. Be clear that you will not consider or be considered as the next full-time preacher.

Two critical agreements:

> Any criticism of Jerrie Barber will be directed to Jerrie Barber, and it will be welcomed. Jerrie Barber does not accept anonymous criticism.

A principle I'll emphasize is delivering mail to the correct person. Matthew 18:15–17 applies to preachers as well as other Christians. I don't respond to, "A lot of people are upset...some people said." I look forward to visiting with each person individually. I appreciate criticism. It helps me grow. I don't accept second-hand criticism.

> It is understood that under no circumstances will Jerrie W. Barber consider or be considered as the next full-time preacher for this congregation.

This is one thing distinguishing interim ministry from fill-in preaching. I'm not here to see if we like each other and to determine if I want to be the next preacher here. I'm not here to take brother Last Preacher's place. I'm here to help the church make a good transition and to make it easier on the next preacher.

See a copy of sample contract in the Appendix.

Chapter 13
How Much Do You Pay an Interim?
What Is Fair Compensation for the Interim Preacher and the Congregation?

In each discussion with a congregation considering inviting me to work with them, we get to the question, "How much do you pay an interim?" My consistent response for nine years, "Pay me what you paid your last preacher."

Five reasons I think this is a good and fair request:

1. You need an interim who's as good at his work as your last preacher was at his.
2. Paying your interim the salary you paid your last preacher is fair for small, medium, and large congregations.
3. You'll pay your next preacher as much, or more than you paid your last preacher. I'll help you hold the place in the budget for him.
4. A worker is worthy of his pay. If an interim preacher has spent his life learning, applying, and teaching the principles of transition, his knowledge and wisdom are

worth that of any other consultant of comparable ability.

5. People show respect, value, and credibility by compensation. Not every church has followed this principle, and I agreed to work with them. Observation: when a church did significantly less, it was also expressed in their attitude toward me. They expressed that by what they paid me and by the way they treated me while I was there. I just wasn't that valuable. Non-verbal communication is powerful. Although I was paid well and lived comfortably, their response to that suggestion was the first sign of how I'd be regarded by them. I'll ponder this in the future.

It's expensive to be an interim.

We live where we work. We've lived in two houses owned by churches for use by their preacher. We've rented two apartments, one house and one duplex, paying utilities on the rented places.

We've maintained our house in Nashville. We pay utilities, property taxes, insurance, and mowing. We don't move to a new location. We live there, bringing our clothes, computers, and an interim bed. Brethren loan us furniture while we're working in a location. They pick it up when we leave. What isn't loaned, Gail buys at a thrift store. This helps the most unpleasant part of our interim ministry, relocating every eighteen months.

God has been good and provided for our every need and most of our wants. I appreciate the support of brethren to permit the enjoyable work we've been doing.

Chapter 14
"I Don't Think We Need to Write It!"
Objections to Written Working Agreements

"We don't need to write anything down. We'll just trust each other like Christians, and I promise you we'll take care of you and work out any problems that come up along the way." And that's been the beginning of disappointing "agreements" between leaders and their new preacher.

But what could go wrong when we're all sincere, honest, and faithful brethren?

Let me suggest a few things I've learned from the University of Hard Knocks, whose colors are black and blue and the school yell is, "OUCH!".

Some possible agreements:
1. What do you expect of me?
2. What are my responsibilities?
3. How will I know if I am doing well, mediocre, or if I am in danger of being terminated?
4. Will I know that in advance of termination or will I be informed on the way out?

5. What spiritual support will I receive?

6. How often and when will I meet with the shepherds?

7. As your preacher, how many weeks do I get for vacation?

8. Will these be with or without pay?

9. How many weeks do I have for workshops and gospel meetings?

10. Who arranges for speakers when I am gone and who pays them?

11. Are there provisions for medical and life insurance, car mileage reimbursement, provisions for continuing education or lectureships or seminars, reimbursement for half of social security, retirement, or other benefits?

12. When I decide to leave, or you decide for me to leave, will there be severance compensation until I relocate?

13. How long will that be?

14. Etc., etc., and etc.

If any, all, or some of those are discussed, how many in the group remember them fifteen minutes after we agreed on them?

In the last two chapters, I wrote about the importance of specific written agreements. Not everyone agrees with that concept. Here are reasons people have for resisting.

"If we don't trust each other any more than that, we have no business working together." It isn't a matter of trust, it's a result of imperfect memory. When you fail to record agreements, a week or five years later, two or more people may have different memories of the facts. After that, each will regard the other with suspicion and distrust. Each is sure he remembered correctly. A way to eliminate that is to write it, sign it, distribute it to all parties, scan it, save it on your computer, back it up to external hard drives (I use three in rotation), secure it in the cloud, and put the original in your safe-deposit box in the bank. Since I've done that, I've never had a disagreement on details of my agreements that wasn't solved by reading the document.

"In my Daddy's day, people just shook hands and did what they said they were going to do." If it worked for your Daddy, I'm pleased. My experience is I forget. We had written agreements with our children when they were growing up. Every time I remember having a disagreement, I was wrong. I wasn't trying to cheat my children. I forgot the details. When we checked the document, I had no trouble doing what I promised to do.

"I don't think it's spiritual for brethren to have to write every detail. It seems like Christians should be able just to agree and do what they said they'd do." God didn't think it was unspiritual to write agreements. In His two big agreements, the Old Testament and the New Testament, He chose to have details and stories recorded in writing. Some of the big agreements, He wrote in stone — twice! When the first copy was deleted by breakage, He had another copy made and placed in a safe-deposit box (the Ark of the Covenant).

My conclusion: the only people who don't need to write their agreements are those who'll never forget and who'll never die — and they need to work only with people who'll never forget and never die. Otherwise, misunderstandings, hurt feelings, and damaged relationships are likely.

Chapter 15
How Do You Get the Word Out?
How Do People Know You Would Like To Work as an Interim?

––––––––––––––––––

Someone asked a few months ago how to get the word out that you're available. Unless a preacher is independently wealthy, which I'm not, it's scary to begin working with congregations, resigning before you get started — effective in eighteen months, and then start the process again.

God has blessed Gail and me since May 2007 to be involved in this ministry. Here's my story:

1. When I thought about the concept, I began to talk to anyone who would listen, and probably some who wished they didn't have to listen.

2. John Parker and I started a monthly newsletter *When Your Preacher Leaves: Interim Services for Churches Between Ministers* in June 2006. We had articles relating to interim ministry, books that were helpful, and a report of our activities during the month. John started interim ministry earlier than I did.

3. Barber Clippings was a blog I started in December 2006. You can start a blog without any expense or spend some money and add more features.

4. Jill Parker built a website for me. It worked well until it needed to be changed. I contacted a company that built a website and instructed me how to maintain it.

5. John and I ended our newsletter in October 2014.

6. I started my blog, *New Shepherds Orientation*, in January 2015. I use a WordPress theme. Michael Hyatt has a helpful video for people wanting to set up a WordPress blog: *How to Launch a Self-Hosted WordPress Blog in 20 Minutes or Less: A Step-by-Step Guide.* I don't think I finished in twenty minutes, but I was able to set it up and have continued to maintain it. New Shepherds Orientation is aimed toward elders, men who want to be elders, and those who love and appreciate elders. Between Preachers deals specifically with interim ministry and has been helpful in getting connected with congregations who consider my services. It's my impression that elders usually spend considerable time on my website before giving me the first call. They have the opportunity to learn more about the concept of interim ministry, and become better acquainted with me. I have an About page, listing my previous works,

family, hobbies, and interests. I have a page with references and letters of recommendations.

7. I choose to be active on Facebook. I communicate blogs posts, book "mustard seeds," meetings, workshops, and the times I've been available for interim ministry. I have a New Shepherds Orientation page where I share information on leadership workshops and ideas on interim ministry. I'm grateful for the amount of free advertisement available by internet, social media, email, and other web-based tools.

8. I'm on Twitter: **@JerrieWBarber.**

9. There've been two times in eleven and a half years that I didn't have a congregation interested when I completed an interim. These two times my habit of adding people and facts to my Contacts paid off. As of today, I have 5,985 entries in my Contacts list on my iPhone. Not everyone in my list has an interest in my interim ministry — plumbers, electricians, mechanics, doctors, etc. But many of them do have an interest. I composed an introductory letter about my work. I went through my list in alphabetical order sending out individual emails — many with personal comments — to people I thought might know of some congregation that could use my service. The first time, in January 2010, I sent out 700 emails. I stayed up one entire night sending out emails. The second time, July 2013, I sent out an even 1,000 emails.

These are some of the ways I have "put out the word" about my availability. This may sound complicated, but it started a quarter of a century ago with talking about an idea I thought would be helpful. I found other people who had the idea before I did who had studied and developed principles I could learn and adapt. The steps that followed were months and years apart. As I view the process, I can say I believe Paul when he wrote, "And my God shall supply all your needs according to His riches in glory by Christ Jesus" (Philippians 4:19).

I'm receiving more and more calls for this work. For those interested, I have conducted a three-day training session on interim ministry. I'm considering doing another. Please contact me if you would like to know more: jerrie@barberclippings.com.

Chapter 16
Beginning an Interim Ministry at a New Church:
My First Three Rules: Clear Expectations Reduce Conflict and Disappointment

---

I like to begin with rules — guidelines, expectations. Family rules are usually unconscious, unspoken, understood, and contradictory. That means we rarely think about them, and neglect discussing them. But when someone violates a family (group) rule, he's in trouble! The group will discipline or shun a rule-breaker.

I think there's a better way. Let's discuss how we're going to relate to each other. What do you expect of me? Let me tell you what I expect of you. Let's negotiate. Then let's hold each other accountable for what we agreed to do.

Some tell me they don't like rules. But we still have them. There are things we like, things we don't like, things we'll tolerate, and things we won't tolerate. It's good to know them. The Golden Rule (Matthew 7:12) is a rule, a good rule.

My second Sunday in a new interim, I begin with my rules, expectations. I explain these same three guidelines in meetings and workshops.

1. Try not to learn very much. This has been my aim since graduating from college and not having to take tests. When I read a book, attend a seminar or lecture, or listen to a podcast, I try not to learn much. I usually can't recreate the outline. I probably missed several points.

Although I try not to learn very much, I want to get something helpful to make a difference in the way I think, act, and relate to God and others. I call it the "mustard seed" principle. Jesus told His apostles if they had faith of a grain of mustard seed, they could move a mountain (Matthew 17:20).

2. You have permission to sleep. I don't know how much sleep you've had. I don't know what kind of medicine you're taking. I don't know how hard you've worked. Sometimes people nod and even take a nap when I'm speaking. I won't be offended.

It used to bother me. I thought it was an insult to my preaching. But you can learn many things from the Bible. In Acts, chapter 20, a man was preaching. A young man went to sleep, fell out a window, and died. Who was the preacher? Paul.

Good preacher or bad preacher? Good preacher. Someone going to sleep doesn't necessarily mean the preaching is bad.

We can gain wisdom from reflecting on our experiences. I started preaching when I was sixteen years old. One Sunday, in November 1962, I was preaching at the Wolf Creek Church of Christ, in Hickman County, Tennessee. I was about halfway through the sermon. I said, "In Hebrews 10:24, 25, we read..." I fell to the floor. I went to sleep during my own sermon. Two doctors examined me and came to the same conclusion: I was exhausted. I'd played a basketball game Friday night. Both teams kept a full-court press going the whole game. My father was building a rock house. I hauled rocks all day Saturday. I went bowling Saturday night. I arose early Sunday morning to study. About halfway through the sermon, it was time for a nap, and I took one.

As I've thought about this, if I sleep when I preach, I shouldn't be upset if other people sleep when I preach.

3. Feel free to use the wastebasket. We'll have someone to empty it at the end of each session. I like to put a filter on the wastebasket — the Bible. If God said it, don't throw it away. And we'll be reading much of God's word. However, there'll be times when I say, "I think; it's my observation; this is the way I see it."

I think it's pretty good. But you may not think it's worth taking home. Feel free to use the wastebasket.

In announcing these three expectations, I'm recognizing what people are going to do anyway. What I've promised is I'm not going to get upset and angry.

I won't be giving tests. The Lord will do that. I'd rather a person get one concept that moves him closer to the example of Jesus than to be able to recite every point.

People may nod or sleep. That's their condition or choice. I won't be monitoring the situation and making loud noises to keep them awake. Each person can be responsible for himself.

A person may disagree with me. If he asks, I'll explain. If he persists, my reply, "This sounds like this may be wastebasket material to you."

Some tell me they don't like rules. But we still have them. There are things we like, things we don't like, things we'll tolerate, and things we won't tolerate.

I'm working on defining myself and letting the church know what I expect and what responses I'll give to different situations.

Chapter 17
Name Memory Rule
What Happens When I Don't Remember Your Name?

I've been preaching since June 1961. We've been doing interim since May 2007. We've worked with eight congregations. There are more than 4,600 people who attend those congregations. Frequently, when I'm in a group, someone will ask, "Do you know who I am?" The answer is often in the negative. The situation is awkward. Embarrassment is felt by both sides of the conversation.

I've found letting people know in the beginning about how I remember names is helpful.

I know how to remember names.

I've been through the Dale Carnegie course five times. I was a student the first time in Madisonville, Kentucky starting in August 1969. Besides the Bible courses I took in college, the Dale Carnegie course is one of the most helpful learning experiences in improving my preaching, study, and working with people. After graduating from that course, I served as a graduate assistant four times. I also took the Dale Carnegie Sales course.

I know how to remember names.

The laws of memory are:
I — *impression*, R — *repetition*, A — *association*

Six common ways to make associations:
B — *business*
R — *rhyming word*
A — *appearance*
M — *meaning*
M — *mind picture*
S — *similar name*

I know how to remember names. I can quote the rules.

However, I often forget to practice what I know. Therefore, I don't remember a couple hundred or more new names quickly.

Let me ask you — do you enjoy someone coming to you, putting you on the spot, and asking, "Do you know who I am; do you remember my name?" I've asked that question to 2,500+ people and I haven't had one person raise a hand indicating they welcome that encounter.

It's encouraging to me. Because no one likes that, I know how everyone is going to treat me. We are followers of Jesus. Jesus taught us how to treat people in the Sermon on the Mount: "Therefore, whatever you want men to do to you, do also to them, for this is the Law and the Prophets" (Matthew 7:12).

My rule is this: If you won't ask me what your name is, I won't ask you what I preached two weeks ago.

If you're in a hurry for me to remember your name, I've found that having a meal with someone improves my memory. Feel free to schedule that soon and let's get acquainted.

Please tell me your name until I repeat it without prompting.

This has worked well. It's true. I'm a slow learner. I don't like to embarrass myself and others. People have understood and cooperated.

I'm doing this for myself. But I'm also doing this for the next preacher. In some congregations where I've worked as an interim, most people don't remember a new preacher coming. Their former preacher had been there many years and knew everyone. It'll be easier on the new preacher if people don't put pressure on him to remember their names the first week.

Chapter 18
Communication Rules
How Will Each Know What the Other Is Thinking?

I was just beginning my ministry at a congregation, shaking people out of the building on a Sunday night. A sister came to me, shook my hand, and roared, "I've been sick two weeks, and nobody came to see me — not even the preacher!" I was surprised and embarrassed. I was surprised because I didn't know she'd been sick. I was embarrassed because she said it in front of several other members. I was trying to get off to a good start in my new work.

I asked her if her doctor knew she was sick. She said he did. I wondered how he found out. She said she told him. I replied, "That's the only way the good Lord gave me to learn things."

About seven years later, I didn't think my salary had kept up with my expenses. It hurt my feelings because the elders hadn't given me a bigger raise.

"What did the elders say when you told them?"

Well, I didn't tell them. I thought elders ought to know things like that. That makes relationships complicated — when we expect people to read our minds.

Paul wrote:

> For what man knows the things of a man except the spirit of the man which is in him? Even so no one knows the things of God except the Spirit of God (1 Corinthians 2:11).

You don't know what I think unless I tell you. I don't know what you think unless you tell me.

I hope no one fails to ask for what they need, then I fail to do what I didn't know they wanted me to do, and they want me to feel guilty. I hope this doesn't happen. If it does, I won't cooperate by feeling guilty.

My commitment to you: I'll tell you what I think will be helpful:
1. From the Bible.
2. From my experience and observations.
3. Remember the waste basket is always available.

My request of you: Please tell me how I can be helpful to you.

Tell me when you are sick, if you want me to know. Tell me if you'd like a visit or, if you'd rather I pray for you and not visit.

In my early ministry, I visited everyone in the local hospital every day, twice if they were very sick, and three times if they were dying. You didn't want to see me the third time the same day. That was a bad sign.

On surgery day, I came to the hospital before a person received a "happy shot" and we prayed. I sat with the family during surgery. After the person was out of surgery, I went to the room, had a prayer; then I left the hospital...until a day in Dalton, Georgia. Marlene Griggs approached me one Sunday morning and said, "Jerrie, Bob's having knee surgery Tuesday. I'd appreciate it if you would NOT come to the hospital and sit with us during surgery."

I was shocked. How could I break my rule?

She continued, "You know how anxious I am. I don't want to have to entertain someone. I'll have my *Reader's Digest*. Steve, Carol, and Leigh Ellen will be there. Are you going to be in town Tuesday?"

I replied I planned to be in town.

Marlene continued her communication, "We expect everything to go well. But, if something bad were to happen, would you come to the hospital?"

I told her I would.

Marlene said, "I appreciate it. If I need you, I'll call you."

Wow!!! What good communication. I began to reflect on my previous practice. I wonder how many times I've bothered people by my presence when they'd rather I'd been somewhere else.

I now have a new policy: please tell me how I can be helpful in any circumstance. I'll try to cooperate.

When I was serving as an interim at the Collegeside congregation, I met the best communicator in Cookeville, Tennessee — Dawn Reeves. The Sunday I explained my Communication Rule, Dawn came to me after services and said, "My name is Dawn Reeves. When I have an operation, I want you to visit me, and I want you to bring chocolate. I don't have any surgery scheduled, but when I do, please visit and bring chocolate."

And it came to pass before I left Cookeville, Dawn Reeves had surgery. I visited and brought chocolate. Why did Dawn Reeves receive chocolate from me when others didn't? Because she asked for it. She is an excellent communicator.

I encourage us to follow Dawn's example. There would be less disappointment if we told people what we wanted from them.

I use electronic communication. I am active on Facebook. I post a "thought of the day" on Twitter. I email and text.

I won't ask anyone to connect on Facebook while I serve as an interim in this congregation. I will confirm anyone who requests me to be a friend on Facebook.

Anyone from this congregation who follows me on Twitter, I'll follow.

I use email and text to communicate facts such as time and place to have lunch. I don't do counseling, Bible studies, or try to settle disagreements by text or email. For those, I like to look someone in the eye. I'll be glad to set a time and place by text or email.

Chapter 19

Criticism Rule
A Leader Is More Like a Lightning Rod Than a Cute Wall Decoration

---

My rule for criticism is: I love criticism! As a young preacher, I dreaded, feared, and avoided criticism. I equated it with failure. I should be able to study enough, work enough, visit enough, and be good enough so people would have nothing but appreciation for me and my work.

I had a conversion experience with a counselor that changed my attitude toward criticism.

One Sunday, I'd received some stinging words. I made an appointment with James Jones, a counselor from the Atlanta area, who worked in our building at Central in Dalton, Georgia, the following day.

I wanted him to do two things:

1. Agree I was right and those who criticized me were wrong. To me, it was clear. I was right. There was no reason for their criticism.

2. I hoped, but doubted, that on one of his visits to our congregation he might work it into his conversation to these people that it was hurtful to me for them to criticize me. It'd be good if they wouldn't do it again.

I presented my case, awaiting his agreement, help, and encouragement.

He paused, as he often did, glanced at me a time or two, then said, "Did it ever occur to you not everybody likes Jerrie Barber?".

Then I paused. That wasn't the reply I expected and wanted. I had nothing to say.

James continued:

Not everybody likes Jerrie Barber. Not everybody has liked Jerrie Barber in the past. Not everybody likes Jerrie Barber today. Not everybody will like Jerrie Barber in the future. That's facts. That's reality. That's the way the world operates. You have two choices:

You can communicate verbally and nonverbally you don't like and don't want criticism. Few will criticize you — until they get ready to fire you. (That wasn't good. I'd experienced that. I didn't like that option. I looked forward to the next.)

You can let people know you're concerned; you want to know what they think and feel. If you communicate clearly, sincerely, and often, they'll tell you. And many times it'll really hurt. But...you'll learn things you'll never learn any other way.

The conversation made sense and made a difference. From then, I've grown in welcoming and inviting criticism. It's a Biblical concept:

Whoever loves instruction loves knowledge, But he who hates correction is stupid (Proverbs 12:1).

I started conducting a *What Do You Think About the Preacher Night* once a year in full-time work. I do a session or two in interim ministry. After services, I set the structure for good discussions, then open the floor for people to tell me how I can improve. The Discussion Rules will be in a later chapter.

During this interchange, I promise to do three things:

1. I'll listen to what's said.
2. I'll write it down.
3. I'll think about it.

I've received some helpful suggestions. I show I'm willing to listen to criticism and not get defensive. I set a precedent. I encourage people to come to me at any time to tell me how to improve. I believe anyone who finds salmonella in my refrigerator and tells me about it isn't hurting me. He's helping me.

Once I invite people to tell me how I can be better and do better, it takes the sting out. When they do, and I thank them, I gain credibility, and often build better relationships. I sometimes write personal notes to those who do an outstanding job criticizing me — especially if it seemed difficult for them.

There's a modification to this rule: I don't accept written anonymous criticism. I won't receive and act on second-hand criticism. Since 2011, I've this in my working agreement: "Any criticism of Jerrie Barber will be directed to Jerrie Barber and it will be welcomed. Jerrie Barber does not accept anonymous criticism." Interim Minister — Transition Consultant Working Agreement, last page.

That means should anyone approach me saying, "We've had some complaints about...", I reply, "I don't accept anonymous criticism. Please have the person or persons talk to me. I'll treat them with respect and appreciation."

Should a person persist (which I haven't experienced), I'd reply, "I cannot respond. It'd be going against my agreement." It'd also be going against scripture. Jesus told us to bring any complaint against a brother by going to him ALONE. (Matthew 18:15).

A leader is more like a lightning rod than a cute wall decoration. A lightning rod rises above the building, saying, "Hit me, hit me." The potentially destructive charge is transferred to the ground. The building is protected. Leadership, greatness isn't for cuteness and admiration. It comes with service and often pain (Matthew 20:25-28).

I communicate this information the fourth week in a new interim. About this time, I conduct a one-hour workshop on Criticism. After this, people test whether I meant what I said or not. Depending on my response, I have the opportunity to increase or decrease my credibility.

But that happens to any leader, whether he articulates the way he handles criticism or not.

Chapter 20
Originality Rule
I Make No Claims to Originality

When I started preaching at the age of 16, I'd never heard of exegesis or hermeneutics. I saw a book at the *Gospel Advocate* Bookstore on expository preaching and thought it was when you wanted to preach a sermon and expose someone for doing something wrong. I bought a sermon outline book, *Simple Sermon Outlines*, by J. C. Choate and used many of the outlines for my sermons during my last two years of high school. It never occurred to me I was plagiarizing. The book was printed to use for Bible study and presentation.

The issue becomes a problem when a preacher claims borrowed material is his. It becomes a problem when a preacher or teacher does little or no Bible study on his own but only copies someone else's material and presents it as his own.

I make no claims of originality. I was born ignorant. I didn't know my A, B, C's or how to count. Everything I know I learned from someone else.

Most of my sermons and classes came from others' books, sermons, articles, and commentaries. One series of nine lessons I prepared from an idea in one sentence in one book which I heard on cassette tapes. I don't remember the book. I don't remember the author.

I may preach one or two sermons from *sermoncentral.com*. I claim no originality. My definition of originality is: "I forgot where I learned it."

There'll be times when I'll give the source. There'll be times when I don't remember the source. If you want to know where I got my information, I'll tell you if I remember.

If I say I read it, I read it. I may not be able to prove it's true.

When I say something happened to me, it happened to me. I won't tell illustrations or jokes as if they happened to someone else if I don't know it happened to them.

When I use the phrase "less than fifty years ago, and less than five hundred miles from here" it means it happened, but I won't disclose the people involved.

My commitment to you is I'll continue to read, study, and listen to present sermons and classes I think will be helpful for us at the time. I learned from someone else. If you want to know my sources, ask. If I know, I'll tell you.

Chapter 21
Discussion Rules
Guidelines for a Peaceful and Productive Meeting

"You can't have a congregational meeting here. It always gets out of hand." "I'd be afraid to address these things with the church. You can never tell what people may say in a group." And so we do not communicate. People are already frustrated because we haven't communicated. We decide not to communicate because people are frustrated. Then they get more frustrated because we are not communicating.

Many discussions, classes, and especially meetings where there is conflict, break up and/or become unproductive. It may be that the leader(s) did not know the value of guidelines.

Amos asked, "Can two walk together, unless they are agreed?" (Amos 3:3). We don't have to agree on everything. But if we are going to travel together from Nashville, Tennessee, to St. Louis, Missouri, we must agree on some things: What time will we leave? What kind of transportation will we take? Who will drive? The clothes we wear and the food we eat along the way can be individual choices, but we must agree on the basics of the trip.

Often "family rules" are unconscious, unspoken, understood, and contradictory.

That means we rarely think about the rules, usually don't discuss them, but people pay a price when they disobey them. It's my observation that it's better to have our rules conscious, spoken, and understood. Then we can evaluate them and change them if that would be helpful to the group: family, congregation, work group, or sports team.

I use a form of these guidelines anytime I am leading a group: counseling, workshop, auditorium Bible class, preachers' workshop stress session, congregational "Family Meeting," or conflict resolution. Many conflicts arise because we are playing by different rules.

I'll discuss the ideas behind the guidelines. James Jones introduced these concepts to me. I watched him in counseling sessions, classes, and leadership workshops. It was amazing how stress went down when I knew the boundaries. It was safe when I played by the rules and believed that others would do the same or be held accountable for not doing so.

These guidelines need to be negotiated – not commanded. Simply reading them to a group will not get a buy-in. I like to discuss them and talk about why they contribute to group health. I take about ten minutes with a group where most of the people are familiar. I take about an hour and a half to negotiate these guidelines when doing a Saturday church meeting during a conflict intervention workshop.

• **May I be the leader of this group?** I need the group's permission because I only lead those who give me permission to be the leader. I may have the authority. My name may be on the brochure or church letterhead as preacher, elder, or Bible class teacher. But if the group doesn't give me permission to be the leader, I will not lead. How much authority does Jesus have (Matthew 28:18)? How many people is He leading? Jesus is only leading those who give Him permission to be their leader. Many are invited, but only those who desire to take the water of life follow Him (Revelation 22:17). He wanted Jerusalem to follow Him and enjoy His protection. But they were not willing (Matthew 23:37). I don't have the authority of Jesus. I will not be the leader if the group doesn't give me permission.

• **Will we start on time?** We penalize those who come on time when we wait for late-comers.

• **Will we quit on time?** Especially in a workshop setting, this helps the group learn to operate within limits, boundaries. That is the way the world operates. It is a good practice since it respects everyone's time.

• **Will we speak one at a time?** (1 Corinthians 14:27–33) If we are working as a group, I show disrespect to the group in general and to the person speaking in particular when I begin a private conversation with my neighbor. If it relates to the group, it should be shared with the group. If it doesn't relate to the group, it can be held until a break.

This has been the most difficult rule for me to enforce as a leader. I have been leading the Third Monday Workshop stress session made up of preachers, elders, youth ministers, and other interested Christians in the Nashville, Tennessee, area since the fall of 1988. Three times I've come to the group to suggest that we agree to dispense with this guideline because it is violated so often. It's embarrassing for me to call to account preachers and elders who are older than I am and have more education than I have for talking when they have agreed not to talk. But each time the group has assured me that it's important to the group process. We still have the guideline, and it seems that it has been observed better for several months.

• **Will we talk where others can hear or will we speak softly and in small groups where others will not know what is being said?** This is a follow-up on the previous guideline. Unauthorized sub-grouping will destroy the group. It drains energy and attention when some obviously do not think the person who is speaking has anything as valuable to say as what they are saying.

• **Will each person speak for himself or herself or will we speak for others such as "they," "them," "everybody," and for God as well?** How many times have you heard, "A lot of people are upset," "Several are unhappy with the preacher"? When asked for names, the reply often is, "Well I can't tell you who they are, but there's a bunch." I like to have the guideline, "I'll speak for me, you speak for you, and let God speak for God. Unless you have been elected to the House of Representatives or the Senate, you don't have permission to represent anyone in this group except yourself." I don't know who the "several" are. I don't know how many are in a "bunch." I'd be interested in knowing what you think. I'll value what you say.

• **Will we have a right to all our feelings: the painful as well as the pleasant?** Some people are convinced that there are good feelings and bad feelings. I think there are pleasant feelings and painful feelings. But it's my understanding that all our emotions are given to us by God and are good for us. I need to be responsible how I act on my emotions, but they're all helpful. I usually mention the four "feeling groups": mad, sad, glad, scared.

We can be sad. We have tissues. If Jesus can cry (John 11:35), I can cry. We can be scared and talk about that. We have a right to be angry. Jesus was angry (Mark 3:5). Therefore, it must not be sinful. Paul said to be angry and not sin (Ephesians 4:26). You have a right to be angry. You have a right to be angry with me. You can talk about being angry with me. However, you do not have a right to hit me or tear up the furniture. There's a difference in what we feel and what we do with our feelings. We can be glad and laugh. There's a qualification on that which is included in the next guideline.

• **Do you want to have a rule that we'll not make fun of what people say in this group?** We can laugh with people but not at people. How can we know if we are laughing with or laughing at? The first test is to see if the other person is laughing. I cannot laugh with someone who is not laughing. But I may need to ask the person being discussed if it feels like we are laughing with him or at him. Solomon said, "Sorrow may hide behind laughter, and happiness may end in sorrow" (Proverbs 14:13, *The Contemporary English Version*). This brings us to the next rule.

• **May I, as a leader, have a right to interrupt?** If I have any question, I'll ask the person who is the focus of the laughter, "Does it feel like we are laughing with you or at you?". Several years ago, I was leading a group. After an elder's wife had made a comment, someone said, "That's the way Yankees are." The group laughed. I asked her, "Does it feel like we are laughing with you or at you?". She replied: "We've been living here fourteen years and worshiping with this congregation. We've taught Bible classes. We've been involved in the work. It'd feel good to be just a Christian, a member of this church and not a 'Yankee Christian.'" We learned a lesson that night.

• **Will we have a right to disagree with each other?** In several decades of leading groups, I've always gained permission for disagreement in the group. I've always said that if I ever get a group where we can't disagree, I want to talk first because I like my opinions better than those of anyone else. But I wouldn't learn very much.

• **Will we settle group business in the group or will we get in small groups afterward and talk about each other?** Polarizing begins to take place when we start talking about each other instead of to each other. If it's group business, it needs to be addressed in the group.

• **Do we want to have a rule of confidentiality: what we say here stays here?** This is essential if we're to develop a trusting group. Many people assume that elders, preachers, and other leaders will keep confidences. This is where people are often hurt. Assuming is not good communication. Too often

Christians don't keep personal matters confidential. I like to talk about it. What does it mean "What we say here stays here"? What if we discuss the weather or read John 3:16 in the group? Can we not take that out of the group? In our staff meetings at Berry's Chapel, we developed the "church bulletin rule": if we talk about something in a staff meeting that we'd print in the church bulletin, we can talk about it out of the group. If we wouldn't print it in the bulletin, we won't carry it out of the meeting. If there's any question, it's best to check with the person or people to whom the information belongs.

• **Will I take care of myself, telling the group only what I trust them to keep?** After we've established this rule, I encourage new members to doubt as long as they need to doubt it. Anyone can say what we've just said, "What we say here stays here." I believe that faith grows through "creative doubt." Creative doubt is doubt that asks questions and sincerely wants to know the truth. It's my observation that it took about two years in our Third Monday Workshop to establish trust in the group where we could talk about serious, personal issues. After establishing that trust in the core group, new members don't seem to diminish the readiness of group members bringing up what they need to discuss. Since August of 1988, I don't know of a matter getting out of the group. That's powerful! That's encouraging to have that kind of support group.

• **If what I say offends or hurts you, will you tell me or will you talk about me to others?** This is a powerful commitment! Think how assuring it'd be if we didn't have to wonder how we were coming across to others.

• **If, after a group session is over, you realize that you didn't get finished, will you bring the matter back to the group and work it out?** This reminds us that we deal with group business in the group.

• **May we be humble instead of arrogant?** That is, if we don't know what someone is thinking or feeling, will we ask or will we assume that we know what they are thinking or feeling? (Matthew 5:3; 1 Corinthians 2:11)

One of my mistakes in communication is attempting to mind-read. I think I know what you're thinking and act on that assumption. The problem is I don't know what you're thinking unless you tell me. The best policy is to ask.

• **May others respond to what we say?** Do I have to have the last word or would it be helpful to get feedback?

• **When we ask a question, will we be willing to tell why we want to know the answer?** I may want to know why someone is asking questions. What are you going to do with the information? Why are you interested?

• **May a person decide to quit talking when they choose?** In most groups, I don't require people to talk. Some people learn better with their mouths open and others learn better with their mouths closed. Each person can decide which works best for them without pressure.

• **Will we attend all sessions? If we must be absent, will we tell the group why?** It's a matter of courtesy to be responsible to a group (class, elder's meeting, committee meeting). It takes energy away from group process when a member is late or absent without explanation. "I wonder if they're sick, had an accident, forgot, or don't care about our work?" This can be eliminated by a call, text, or e-mail: "I'll be fifteen minutes late," or "I'm sick and unable to attend tonight's meeting."

• **Will we agree not to talk about group business during breaks?** This guideline is especially helpful in groups that are learning experiences in how groups work. If we talk about group business during breaks, we deprive the rest of the group of our thoughts and ourselves of the wisdom of the rest of the group. If the meeting is dealing with conflict, it's easier to choose sides and plot destruction by subdividing and talking about others during breaks of ten minutes or two days.

• **While in the discussion and exploration of new ideas, will the group allow any title, position, seniority, family relationship, age, actual or perceived net worth, chain of command, or level of management, inhibit or repress any comment or idea from being shared and seriously considered?** When this principle is ignored, many times a "head elder" will result. This may be a toxic head elder or a benevolent head elder. I think both are hurtful to the long-term leadership of the church or any group.

• **Are we aware that some of these rules will probably be broken? What will we learn about ourselves and leadership when they are broken?**
   a. By us?
   b. By others?

Can we ask and will we answer the question, "What did you learn from that"? These guidelines form boundaries that are sometimes difficult to remember and keep. When we hold ourselves and others accountable to do what we agreed to do, it can be helpful. If a guideline isn't helpful, it can be changed. Self-reporting is especially commendable and an opportunity to teach and give others permission to analyze themselves in the group process.

•**Will we agree to try to apply these Biblical principles to ourselves before we try to "fix" other people who are in this group or people who are not here?** (Psalm 139:23, 24; 1 Corinthians 9:27; 2 Corinthians 13:5; 10:12) It's hard to keep everyone in the room during a class or group session. I want to jump out the window and bring in a friend or an enemy who needs to hear this more than I do. "I wish John and Mary were here. They need to hear this. Those folks down the street need this." I call this the "me first" principle of Bible study. The first question I need to ask when studying God's word or implementing principles that I am learning is, "How does this apply to me?".

• **May we bring up "old business" if we need to clarify or discuss something further?** Sometimes a comment is countered by, "We've already talked about that." If a person isn't finished with an issue, it may need to be discussed again.

• **May we have permission to make additional rules, if needed, to help this group be more effective?**

This list is not exhaustive. Some discussions need fewer guidelines, some more.

In some meetings involving anticipated conflict, we had the "no shouting" rule. As the facilitator, I've been told that previous meetings had ended in a shouting match which was hurtful. It was suggested that I call people to account when they were getting too loud. I decided not to get into the middle of that group's conflict. What we negotiated was that when three people held up their hands when a person was getting louder and louder, I would report to the speaker, "Three people in the group think you are getting louder than is helpful for this discussion." That helps the group be responsible for itself and keeps me out of the middle of a conflict that doesn't belong to me.

In some meetings, we have had the "Why are you leaving?" rule. When I was informed that this group's meetings often end in people leaving mad, we worked out the agreement that if people left, they would tell why. This kept people from assuming that people were leaving angry or letting them know that they were angry and possibly why.

In one preachers' meeting, the group requested the guideline, "We will not talk disparagingly about any person not present." This came out of painful experience of previous preachers' luncheons that developed into a discussion of who was doing or saying the wrong things since our last meeting. This spirit killed that meeting.

Would you be willing to tell what you like about this group process, what's helpful and what's not helpful, and in this way give suggestions for improving future discussions?

This can be one of the most helpful guidelines for the leader as well as for the rest of the group. If the leader is serious and honest, he or she can model a learning attitude that encourages growth. I like criticism! When anyone loves me enough to tell me how I can improve, that person is doing me a favor. If you find salmonella in my refrigerator and tell me about it, you're not hurting me. You're helping me.

When I'm leading a meeting, I have the choice of the Amos rule, "Can two walk together, unless they are agreed?" (Amos 3:3), or the Judges rule, "In those days there was no king in Israel; everyone did what was right in his own eyes" (Judges 21:25). Which rule I choose can make a great difference in the effectiveness of the discussion.

Chapter 22
Opening Family Meeting
An Introduction to Transition and Interim Ministry

At the beginning of each interim, usually on the first Sunday night following evening services, I hold a Family Meeting to get the process started. In two larger congregations, 600 and 1,400 in Sunday morning attendance, I went to Bible classes for this discussion. This provided an opportunity for more people to participate in the discussion.

I begin with the Discussion Rules. I start each new group with negotiating the Discussion Rules: Sunday morning Bible Class, Wednesday night Bible class, Staff Meetings, Transition Monitoring Team. When I had gone over the Discussion Rules the second time in one congregation, a perplexed brother asked, "How many times am I going to have to listen to those rules?".

My reply, "Every time we start a new group. And you haven't heard anything yet. You're on the Transition Monitoring Team. We'll take an hour to negotiate the rules at the first meeting."

During this first Family Meeting, an information session for the entire congregation, we are setting structure and expectations of the next year to year and a half of our work together.

Introduction:
- I tell how we started interim ministry.
- I explain the concept of transition.
- Recruit people for specific transition tasks.
- Transition Monitoring Team: a group to tap into the grapevine of the church and communicate to the elders what people are thinking, feeling, asking, saying, fearing, and hoping.
- Welcome to our congregation and community: a document or part of the website to introduce the prospective preachers to the congregation and the community.
- Timeline of this congregation: a compilation of the history, attendance, and contribution of the congregation from the earliest records until the present.
- Conducting a self-study: an extensive questionnaire to let members tell who they are, evaluate the strengths and needs of the congregation, and describe the type of preacher needed at this church now. This will be set up as an on-line survey with printed copies for those who prefer that to using an electronic tablet or computer.

Planned sermon series:

- Carving Ears, Cutting Out, Calling Angels, or Crucifixion, requirements for a follower of Jesus. Luke 9:23
- How to Survive the Storm and Enjoy the Sunshine, dealing with conflict in the church. Acts 6:1-7
- I Want the Church to Grow, But I Don't Want Any More People, overcoming my discomforts to reach out to people unlike me and people I don't like.
- What Do You Do When God Is Late?, setting my clock with God's clock.
- Workshop once a month on Sunday night, a longer lesson on a practical topic.
- Leadership Training Classes.
- God's Great Servants, conducted on Wednesday night for elders, deacons, other men and young men who desire to be leaders in the church, their family, business, and other areas.

These classes are for the administrative part of leadership.

- Learning to Love My Friend(s), classes in the homes of the participants. We learn to have a greater appreciation of Jesus as my Friend, become a better friend to others using Jesus as the example of a perfect friend, and encourage telling others about our best Friend by word and example. The study is about the pastoral part of leadership.

- Read my working agreement, including my job description, salary and housing allowance — if the elders permit. Early in my ministry, I didn't want people to know my financial arrangements. I've learned that full disclosure of all agreements helps people understand and eliminates many questions. They already have the answers.
- Questions and comments.

Chapter 23
Staff Meetings
Coordinating and Growing Individually and as a Group

Unity isn't an accident looking for a place to happen. I often hear youth ministers, preachers, administrative assistants, and other members of the team talking about either bad or practically non-existent relationships among those who work out of the church building. I ask about their staff meetings, celebrations, and time they spend together. The answer often is, "We don't spend time together."

I'm not surprised that camaraderie isn't great without aiming for it and working for it. I've enjoyed in four of six interim congregations having other people who are part of the team. We've had weekly staff meetings.

These weren't always welcomed. As we began at one congregation, I asked, "What kind of staff meeting would you like to have?"

The reply from more than one person was, "None." They told me previous staff meetings were times when they were reprimanded and embarrassed. I can understand their aversion to that kind of meeting.

In some congregations, we have one or more elders who come to staff meetings. In some, they rotate. In others, it's the same elder each time.

I begin with rules. Family rules are usually unconscious, unspoken, but understood. I spend the first meeting discussing and negotiating rules for staff meetings. I like to discuss them, agree to follow the guidelines we've negotiated, then review them six months from the beginning and adjust to achieve better results.

GUIDELINES FOR STAFF MEETINGS

1. The purposes (reasons) for having staff meetings will be:
   a. To have clear, accurate, and caring communication with each other and to have that same kind of communication transferred to the congregation and to those outside the church as well.
   b. To coordinate schedules for the most effective use of time and talent.
   c. For mutual edification of each other and others.
   d. To grow spiritually through Bible study and prayer.
   e. To work on growing in our effectiveness as a team.
   f. To quickly and positively address and solve problems that arise.

2. The time for staff meetings will be 10:30 A.M. each Monday that the office is open.

3. The time limit will be one hour.

4. We agree that the staff meeting is important. All staff members are expected to be present. That will be shown by placing it on a high priority on our weekly schedule. Only events of the seriousness of funerals, medical emergencies, or problems that cannot be rescheduled without hardship will delay or eliminate staff meetings. When only a part of the staff is involved, the remainder of the staff will continue the meeting. If a staff member is going to be late or absent, she/he will communicate that to the group.

5. Jerrie will coordinate the meetings.

6. Regarding potential interruptions:
   a. We will not receive phone calls during the meeting.
   b. The answering machine will be used during meetings; this will be communicated to the congregation.

7. We recognize that we have a right to all our feelings such as anger, grief, joy, fear, etc., and that we can express those with care, concern, and responsibility.

8. We can disagree as well as agree and can feel free to express our thoughts in a way that values and respects others.

9. We have agreed to speak confidentially during staff meetings. That means that what we say here stays here and will not be shared with others outside the meeting unless it is general knowledge that others would receive from sources other than staff. Material that would not be appropriate to publish in the weekly bulletin is not to be shared with anyone: family, friends, or other members of this congregation or others.

10. We will celebrate and grieve as a group.
    a. Birthdays will receive appropriate recognition.
    b. We will have a time to say good-bye to departing staff members.

11. We have a right to bring up old business when we feel we have not finished with any issue.

12. We agree to change any guideline that needs to be changed – adding, deleting, or modifying any rule that would promote more helpful, productive, and encouraging staff meetings.

13. We will reevaluate our guidelines during our staff meeting six months from today.

There are three parts to our staff meetings:

1. Bible study and prayer. We read a book of the Bible, a chapter a week. We spend about 30 minutes reading and discussing the chapter. The way we select a book to read is to give everyone a piece of paper. Each person indicates the book they would like to read in staff meetings. We draw one suggestion to start, finish it, then draw for the next book. Eventually, everyone gets to study the book he or she suggested.

2. Coordination. We discuss what's going on in the congregation: regular services and projects, special events, the bulletin, people's schedules, and other things that need to be coordinated.

3. Staff development. This consists of reading 3-5 pages from a book encouraging growth in a group of people who work with others. It often takes a year or longer to read a book. But at the end of the year, we have ideas and a vocabulary enabling us to work more effectively. Some of the books we've read in staff meetings:

Leaders Who Last, by Margaret J. Marcuson

Friedman's Fables, by Edwin H. Friedman

Transitions, by Willam Bridges

Managing Transitions, by William Bridges

Generation to Generation, by Edwin H. Friedman

How Your Church Family Works, by Peter L. Steinke

Healthy Congregations, by Peter L. Steinke

Our staff has times of celebrations. We celebrate birthdays. It's the responsibility of the person having a birthday to remind us it's time for a birthday party. We go to a restaurant of their choice. Different groups have their rules on paying for the meal. In some, each person helps pay for the honoree's meal and brings a card for the birthday. In others, elders allot money from the budget to pay for everyone's meal. In one church, we enjoyed birthday parties so much we celebrated half-birthdays. Six months after each person's birthday, he or she alerted us the half-birthday was coming up. We went to a restaurant of their choice; each person paid for their meal, and the honoree brought a birthday card for himself and told why he deserved the card.

It's also good to schedule a time to say good-bye. When a staff member is leaving, we have a meal together and say what we need to say to reflect on our time together. Staff relationships ooze out to the congregation. I believe that health is contagious as well as disease.

When the preacher, youth minister, administrative assistants, and other people who work from the church office, like each other, get along, and work well together, people learn that.

They notice the relationship, appreciate it, and may imitate it in their interactions with those close to them.

The opposite is also true.

It's my observation that time and money spent in developing better staff relationships are wise investments and produce valuable dividends.

Chapter 24
Transition Monitoring Team:
What Are People Thinking, Saying, Asking, Losing, Fearing, and Hoping?

———————

In my first interim, the elders asked for help with communication. They said, "Members won't tell us what they're thinking."

As soon as we arrived, Gail and I started visiting families in the congregation. We asked three questions:

1. What do you like about this congregation?
2. What would you like to see improved?
3. What can we do while we're here to help you?

Ninety percent of families we visited said, "We need help with communication. The elders won't tell us what's going on."

I picked up the idea of a Transition Monitoring Team from William Bridges in his book, *Managing Transitions*. He makes a case for this type of group:

Leaders usually assume that all the feedback they need will come up through regular channels and be voiced at staff meeting in reply to the question, "How are things going?" Such is seldom the case...Ed Carlson, the former CEO of

United Airlines, used to call it the NETMA problem —
"Nobody Ever Tells Me Anything" (pages 48, 49).

I set up the Transition Monitoring Team of twenty people as
soon as I arrive at a new congregation. I want ten volunteers. I
ask the elders to select ten people: five who like you and five
who don't.

It should be clear at the beginning — this is a transition
monitoring team — not a transition management team. This
group has no decision-making authority. Their work is to
report what they're hearing in the congregation.

The first meeting is to go over the purpose of the Transition
Monitoring Team and negotiate Rules of Discussion (Chapter
21). We agree on how we'll conduct ourselves in this role.

There is an emphasis on the rule of confidentiality — what we
say here stays here. I've seen no better illustration of everyone
understanding and participating in this guideline than the
flood wall in Jeffersonville, Indiana. Around the town, the wall
has several places where cars and people can pass through
until the Ohio River starts rising. Then the gaps are filled. Some
are large enough for two cars to pass through. On the sides of
large openings, are small openings the size of a door in our
house. I ask, "How many gaps have to be left open for water to
get into Jeffersonville flooding the town?" The answer is

obvious. In reports of the Transition Monitoring Team, sources of comments and reporters are confidential.

The group meets once a month. We do three things described in an email I send out on Monday preceding the meeting:

Brothers and Sisters,

The next meeting of the Transition Monitoring Team will be Sunday, 5:00 p.m., January 8 in Room 101.

Our agenda:

1. What have you heard from people and how should you respond? As you hear comments, feel free to take notes and bring them to the meeting.

　　a.　What are they saying?

　　b.　What are they asking?

　　c.　What do they fear?

　　d.　What are they losing?

　　e.　What are their hopes?

2. What "mustard seed" did you get from reading Transitions, chapter 5?

3. How are you dealing with this transition and other transitions in your life?

We will be finished in 60 minutes or less.

As can be seen, Transition Monitoring Meetings have three parts:

1. Reporting. What have you heard since the last meeting? Members express what they've heard people say about the church and the transition. No names are attached to the source or the reporter. Members of the Transition Monitoring Team can talk to themselves and report things they think the elders should hear. These results are recorded by a member of the team, typed, and given to the elders after each meeting.

2. Sharing "mustard seeds" of what they're learning. Each member of the team is given a copy of Transitions, by William Bridges. He explains the process of transition. There are predictable steps: an ending, a new beginning, and in the middle a neutral zone where people are confused, blaming, depressed, and wishing we could "get things back like they used to be." When we understand this is expected, we can be less anxious than if we see all these human responses as sinful, dangerous, and indications that things are falling apart. I believe health is contagious as well as disease. This group will come to understand the process. When someone is in despair and saying there's no hope, the team member can understand

and communicate that these feelings are normal. We'll get through the wilderness of the neutral zone and enter the promised land of the new beginning, if we don't lose hope.

3. Personal application. As trust grows in the group, three or four months, people begin to share how much of their church anxiety is tied to anxiety related to personal, family, and business issues. Many tell how principles they learned in the group have been helpful to them in their personal life.

I warn the elders they may be shocked at the first report or two from the Transition Monitoring Team. In churches I've served, most of the shepherds weren't aware of thoughts and feelings of many in their flock.

In one church, one of the elders was a professional counselor in private practice. Monday morning after I'd given the elders the first report from the Transition Monitoring Team, this shepherd-counselor called, "Jerrie, after reading the report of the Transition Monitoring Team, I'm depressed."

My response, "You need a good counselor."

When we know what to expect, we can be less anxious.

There's hope. Jesus said, "And you shall know the truth, and the truth shall make you free" (John 8:32). In the context, Jesus was talking about revealed truth from God. But the principle applies to any part of truth. When you know what people are thinking, feeling, saying, and doing, you can prepare to make an appropriate response.

Chapter 25
Self-Study Survey:
What Kind of Preacher Do We Want?
What Kind of Preacher Will Want Us?

Many Christians have an idea of the characteristics of the preacher they'd like to have. If the last preacher was their good friend, they probably want another just like him. Those aren't available. If they didn't like the former preacher, someone who is exactly opposite him would be good. There are none of those.

Most want a preacher who lives like Jesus, studies like Paul, loves like John (when he was older), and visits and ministers like the Good Samaritan. It's good to know what you are seeking, or you won't know when you find him.

Have you thought about what prospective preachers are looking for in a congregation? How do they know if they fit the opportunities and expectations of the church? Are you aware the church is "trying out" as well as the preacher?

One helpful tool is a Self-Study Survey. I helped congregations administer one of these in each church where I've served as an interim.

There are several parts:

1. Demographics: age, how long with the congregation, travel time to and from services.
2. Involvement: roles, attendance, increase or decrease in involvement and why.
3. Evaluation of programs and services of the congregation.
4. How the congregation is like or different in its makeup compared to the community.
5. Possible tasks of the future preacher and which are most important.
6. Evaluation of the worship of the congregation.
7. Thoughts on what makes a good sermon.
8. Convictions on certain issues.
9. Three open-ended questions:
   a. What would you tell the next preacher at this church?
   b. What advice would you give the elders of this church as they proceed?
   c. Please make any other comments that would be helpful for the health of this congregation during this time of transition or in the future.

The survey is anonymous. We don't ask for names or save IP addresses of computers used.

Most congregations where I served used SurveyMonkey, an online survey tool. Paper copies are available for those who prefer and those who want to think before starting on the computer.

Filling out the survey takes forty-five minutes to an hour. We wanted, and have obtained, at least half the Sunday morning attendance to complete the self-study.

My observations after administering and reading every word of surveys in seven congregations:

- Not everyone thinks alike. Some people who have different understandings are sitting on the pew with me — or very close.
- Christians are at different stages in their growth, understanding, and service.
- People have different expectations of a preacher.
- The results of the survey can help men who are considering and being considered as the next preacher.
- Open-ended questions are powerful. People have an opportunity to say what they've wanted to say. I've seen a change in the way those thoughts were shared. In the first two congregations, answers to the open-ended questions were not shared with the congregation. In the third, a committee summarized and paraphrased the answers to share with the church and prospective preachers. In the last three, answers were shared with the church and prospective preachers. I prefer the latter. The work of the search committee or elders is

not to make the church look perfect, but to let a preacher know the challenges and opportunities before he gets there. This is one way to do this. If this isn't the group he would like to serve, now's the time to learn that. The best time to get a divorce is before you get married.

- From my perspective, the most helpful thing about the survey is the thinking going on in the person completing the survey. Many have never thought of how complex leading and preaching to a group of people can be. Not everyone will get everything they want.

One of the most spiritual things a person can do is to think. One of the differences in fill-in preaching and interim ministry is that the interim minister leads in several planned activities to encourage members to think about themselves and their relationship to the Lord. They also consider the effectiveness of the congregation and how it is serving Jesus, their community, and the world, and the transition going on in this church and their lives.

Chapter 26
Introduction to This Church and Our Community:
Would You Want to Work With This Church and Live in This Community?

The first task of the search committee isn't to hire this great preacher. The main goal of the great preacher isn't to try to be selected by this outstanding congregation. The great question is, "Do we fit?" One step in answering the question is for both to provide as much about themselves as would be helpful.

One way each church where I've served as an interim did this, was to prepare a document giving an introduction to the church and the community.

The first congregation prepared a 3-ring binder. Succeeding churches produced the document digitally on their website or a CD.

Some things included were:

Introduction to the Church
- History.
- Plans and vision of the future.

- Leadership.
- Ministries.
- Statistics of attendance and contribution for several decades.
- Results of self-study survey.

Introduction to the Community
- History.
- Recent census.
- Schools for children and adults.
- Local sports programs.
- Medical facilities.
- Transportation.
- Recreation.
- Other interesting things within driving distance of this community.

The best approach I observed in my ministry was from a church in Texas. I received a call one Monday morning. A gentleman said he would like to meet with me. He needed thirty minutes of my time. We agreed on 4:00 that afternoon.

At 4:00 p.m., two men arrived at my study in Dalton, Georgia. They identified themselves as elders of another church. They had a package of information about the church and community. I informed them I wasn't interested in moving to Texas. They told me, "We're not asking you to move to Texas.

Please consider this information and ask any questions you have. Think and pray about this and see if this is an opportunity you should consider. We'll be in contact with you in a couple of weeks." They had driven from Texas to Georgia to deliver the information. That began a three-month discussion. It was a memorable time of learning how to consider and be considered by a church.

They had a very detailed approach to let us patiently consider each other and whether we should work together.

Several years ago, a church selected a new preacher. He moved and had a great beginning. He helped the church by his preaching. He was serving in a great way. Everything seemed to be perfect. But in a short time he was moving. Why? There wasn't a Walmart nearby and his wife wasn't happy without Walmart.

Those are things you can learn before you select a preacher and save confusion and moving expenses — coming and going.

The information-gathering of the search is important. In addition to the facts we share with each other, we're telling each other the amount about us we're willing to disclose, the excellence and details of the work we do, and how much of what Jesus said we believe:

And you shall know the truth, and the truth shall make you free (John 8:32).

Therefore, whatever you want men to do to you, do also to them, for this is the Law and the Prophets (Matthew 7:12).

Chapter 27
Timeline:
Are We Growing, Plateaued, or Declining?

Before we decide where we want to go, we need to know where we are.

How big is the congregation? "Oh, we run about 250 or 260. Of course, it was Family Day year before last since we hit that number." "It seems like we're gaining a few now. The parking lot looked like there were more cars than usual."

Those statements may or may not correspond to reality.

The best way I know how to learn the facts is to average attendance and contribution for as many years as the church has kept records and plot the results on a graph. Growth or decline is clear. I know nickels and noses are not the whole story, but they're part of the indication of the health of the church.

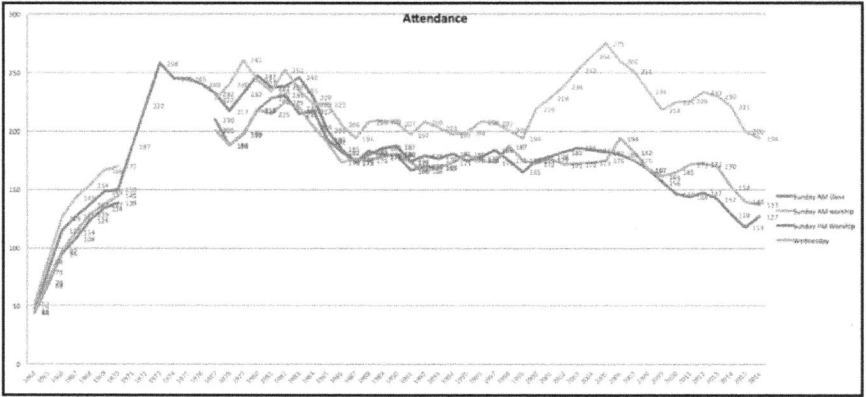

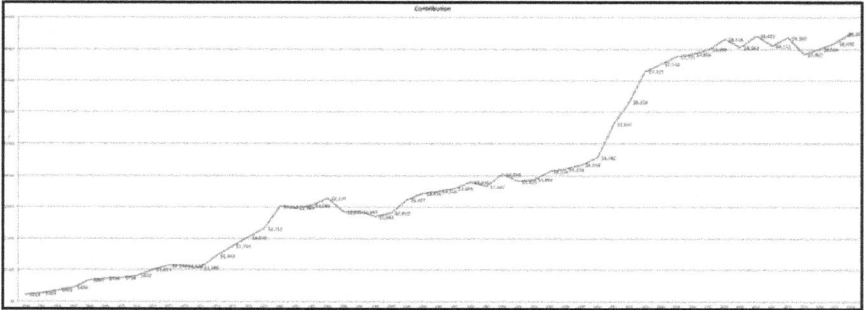

Early in the interim process, I ask for volunteers to collect and record this information. In one congregation, we went through boxes and boxes of old bulletins to assemble figures.

The easiest time of collecting stats was at Eddyville, Kentucky. Emma Walker had kept information for Sunday mornings, Sunday nights, Wednesday nights, gospel meetings, and Vacation Bible Schools since the church moved to "New Eddyville" in 1961.

We copied her hand-written books (I didn't want to be responsible for losing the originals), distributed them to people who transferred information to Excel spreadsheets, and drew charts on large paper.

In other congregations, we made spreadsheets, took them to Staples or Office Depot and printed large charts to display.

Adding other information can help give a visual factual reminder of major changes in the congregation:

- Appointment and resignations or deaths of elders and deacons.
- Names and dates of service of preachers, youth ministers, and other staff members.
- Building programs or relocations of the church.
- Other major events that have affected the congregation.
- Plotting of national and world events can put additional perspective to the graphic history.

After we review and discuss graphs and events, we divide into small groups and encourage people to share their memories of pleasant and painful events in the congregation.

A copy of this timeline should be sent to each preacher the church is considering. Just as the search committee wants a résumé, recordings of sermons, and three references of each preacher they are considering, they should supply information to candidates to help them evaluate their fit in this church.

I've observed the night of the timeline discussion to be a time of celebration, shock, nostalgia, contemplation, and hope. It's one way of helping a group come to terms with its history.

Chapter 28
Learning from Previous Shepherds:
What I See Now, I Wish I Had Known Then

In one interim congregation, I met an unusual number of men who had served as elders. Some were still in the congregation. Others were in the community. Only two were in other cities.

As I was getting acquainted, I kept meeting men who told me, "I used to be an elder here." Or someone else would point to a man as a former shepherd.

After several of these encounters early in my tenure, I said during an elders' meeting, "I think every baptized man in this county has served as an elder of this church at one time or another."

I wondered if we could gain some wisdom by talking with these men. The elders of the church I was serving gave me permission and encouragement, along with names and phone numbers. I was able to interview 26 of 27.

I called for appointments and visited each man. I assured his information would be confidential, not sharing names with specific answers. I was thrilled with the cooperation of former elders and the willingness of the present elders to meet for several hours and discuss these observations.

Questions I Asked

1. How long were you an elder?
2. How was your experience?
   a. Good?
   b. Unpleasant?
3. While you were serving as an elder if you had had a magic wand, what would you have changed to make the eldership better?
4. In what ways and how often did people express appreciation to you for your service?
5. What appreciation did you receive when you resigned?
6. Why did you leave the eldership: personal issues, good of the church, forced?
7. Did you see alliances, division in the eldership?
8. If so, how was this handled?
9. What suggestions do you have for the present eldership?

Observations from Former Elders

1. Of 24 who answered this question, there was a total of 143.58 years of service. Average was 6 years.

2. Good experiences: fellowship with fellow shepherds, better relationship with the congregation, able to know God and people better.

3. Unpleasant experiences: doing the work of deacons, board of directors, some elders did not live up to their word, politicking.

4. Ways to improve shepherd service: fewer decisions — more visiting, change focus from administration to spiritual matters, more shepherding — less firefighting, continue training of elders.

5. What appreciation did you receive for your service?: 81% said they received regular and adequate appreciation while they were serving; 19% said they did not. When they resigned, 50% said they received appreciation, 50% said they did not.

6. Why they left the eldership: moved, frustrated, asked to leave, personal and family issues, burned out, finished what I came to do.

7. 84% said there were alliances and divisions in the eldership when they served. 16% said there were none.

8. Most said alliances were not handled. Several reported there were meetings before meetings to decide what was going to be decided in the meetings.

Answers provided excellent insight gained from Bible study, prayer, experience, and time in reflection.

There were many good suggestions for the present eldership. I am not reporting those. To do so might reveal individuals commenting to some who are in that congregation.

For this process to be effective, the person asking questions and recording answers should do it for information only and not explain, prosecute, or defend present or former elderships.

Consider this, or a similar exercise, to tap the wisdom of men who have served, still love the Lord and His church, and can give good perspectives when asked.

Chapter 29
Preaching During the Interim... Beginning:
Let's Look at Ourselves Before We Start Looking for a Preacher

The aim of this book is to tell how I do interim ministry. There's a better way and I hope to do better the next time. I think I've improved since my last interim. This is the plan for now.

I don't think other interim preachers need to preach the same sermons I preach the same way I preach them. This is a report — not a recommendation.

The first Sunday after moving to a new location is Psalm 118:24. I ask three questions:

- Do you believe Jesus loves His church? Surely. He died for it.
- Do you believe Jesus loves this congregation? Absolutely. Every saved person here is a member of His body, His bride.
- Do you believe God will give us wisdom during this process? He promised it in James 1:5.

The second Sunday in the new church: Recruiting People to Be in the Mustard Seed Collectors and Planters Association. This is an expansion of my first rule: Try not to learn very much. It doesn't take many Christians doing things better to help the church grow and become more healthy.

We pass out Official Mustard Seed Collector and Planter cards:

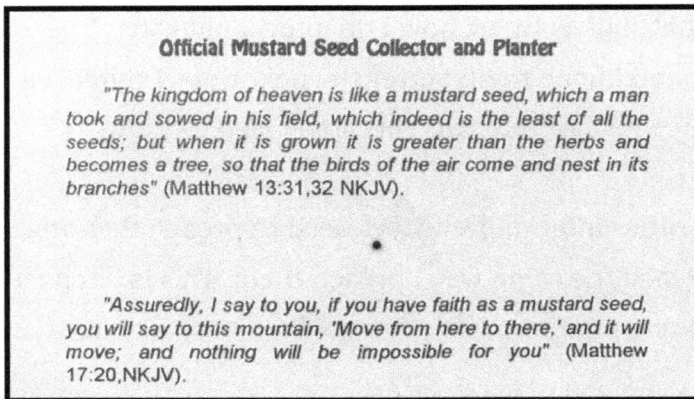

Official Mustard Seed Collector and Planter

"The kingdom of heaven is like a mustard seed, which a man took and sowed in his field, which indeed is the least of all the seeds; but when it is grown it is greater than the herbs and becomes a tree, so that the birds of the air come and nest in its branches" (Matthew 13:31,32 NKJV).

•

"Assuredly, I say to you, if you have faith as a mustard seed, you will say to this mountain, 'Move from here to there,' and it will move; and nothing will be impossible for you" (Matthew 17:20,NKJV).

The next week I start a seven-week series on Luke 9:23:

Then He said to them all, "If anyone desires to come after Me, let him deny himself, and take up his cross daily, and follow Me" (Luke 9:23).

Before we look for a preacher, let's look at ourselves. Are we the kind of church, am I the kind of Christian, who would attract the kind of preacher we would like to have?

Jesus tells us in Luke 9:23 the path to being His disciple, following Him: deny self, take up your cross daily, and follow Jesus. When I want to do something well, I learn best by watching someone who does it well. I believe Jesus was the best cross-carrier Who ever lived. Paul did a good job following Jesus. Jesus and Paul will be our models during this series of how to carry a cross successfully.

You Have the Power to Live Through Dying
How to Be a Good Winner by Losing
Luke 9:23

1. What Choices Do I Have When I Face Difficult Decisions?
2. Why Can't I Have Everything? What Do I Have to Give Up?
3. Will I Always Have Pain in My Life?
4. What Do I Do When I Am Embarrassed to Do Right?
5. How Can I Make Difficult Decisions?
6. How Do I Keep Going When I Want to Give Up?
7. Why Would I Make a Decision to Suffer? What Will I Gain?

This is the first nine weeks on Sunday morning. I want the church to have a good transition. A good transition begins with a good ending. The gospel is the death, burial, and resurrection of Jesus (1 Corinthians 15:1-4). I find many get excited about resurrection. Not many want to volunteer for crucifixion. The truth is: crucifixion precedes resurrection. That's the ending that starts the new beginning.

After nine sermons: two introductions and a series on discipleship from Luke 9:23, I preach a first principle sermon on *Can We Make Progress by Going Backward?*.

The next Sunday, I start a series on How to Survive the Storm and Enjoy the Sunshine. These sermons discuss how to deal with problems in the church.

Chapter 30

Preaching During the Interim... Church Problems:
Why Did We Have Problems in the Church?

How to Survive the Storm and Enjoy the Sunshine

1. **Why Do We Have Problems in the Church and How Long Will They Exist?** We have problems in the church because we have people in the church. How long will we have problems in the church? As long as we have people in the church.

2. **What Other Things Cause Problems in the Church?** Jesus invites and attracts open, habitual, active sinners. When they accept His invitation to follow, they bring problems with them. Old attitudes and habits don't disappear instantly. Jews wanted to continue to observe and bind circumcision and the law of Moses. Some people are slow learners. It took at least three tries for Peter to understand the unity of Jews and Gentiles. When we invite and embrace "whosoever will," the whosoevers bring their problems with them. The problem in many churches is they don't have enough problems. They screen out

undesirables and only accept people who are like them and those they like. This isn't the invitation of Jesus.

3. **What are Some Situations that May Precede Greater Problems?** Many things happened between the church "having favor with all the people" and the first church conflict in Acts 6. Acts 2 begins with a different Pentecost. A new age was coming. People were in Jerusalem from different backgrounds. There was a radical change for some of the converts. They converted from "Let Him be crucified...His blood be on us and on our children" to "Men and brethren, what shall we do?". Lingering visitors placed a strain on finances and hospitality that led to radical fund-raising. The rapid growth—3,000, daily additions, 5,000 men, believers increasingly added, the numbers of the disciples was multiplying—brought opportunity for more problems. Growing churches where I've worked experienced increased problems. Acts 4 brings a new issue: opposition from outside the church. The apostles were arrested and imprisoned. Acts 5 tells of a sin problem within the Jerusalem church. Acts 6 opens with conflict.

4. **How Can Good Communication Help Solve Problems?** My beginning assumption is the apostles were good leaders. Jesus selected them, taught them, and trained them. Their résumé was adequate. When complaint came, they listened. There was a conflict between the Grecian group and the Hebrew group.

We have groups in our congregations: rich-poor, young-old, black-white-brown-yellow, country-city, Democrat-Republican-Independent, your family-my family. Their differences are sometimes bases for conflict. The apostles listened to the murmuring, complaint, quarrel. This isn't good communication. But the widows were being neglected. The apostles didn't wait until everyone passed a New and Improved Communication Class before they moved to help widows. All communication should be heard, evaluated, and an appropriate response given.

5. **Why Am I Often Disappointed in Leaders?** People being disappointed in their leaders doesn't necessarily indicate the leaders are inadequate. Even the best leaders have limitations and blind spots. The apostles were good leaders. However, widows were neglected. Even the best leaders cannot do everything that should be done in a growing church. The apostles essentially said, "We're not going to the grocery store." The benevolent work was good. They weren't the ones to do it. Good leaders won't be pressured into doing a thousand other tasks because of guilt or fear of losing leadership.

6. **How Many People Should Be Involved in Solving Problems?** Good leaders don't assume responsibility which belongs to the group in solving group problems, but they help and lead the group in a solution. The apostles' response: we won't neglect

our responsibility in the ministry of the word and prayer to put out brush fires. You select seven men to lead this effort. We'll appoint them. They'll do the work.

7. How Can Trust Grow Between Leaders and Followers?

Sometimes the congregation doesn't trust the elders and the elders don't trust the congregation. Both have good examples and reasons. If you don't believe it, ask them, and they'll tell you. Someone has to start the trust risk. When people are commissioned to become part of the solution instead of a burden and a problem, they'll be happy. The multitude was pleased (Acts 6:5). Greeks were neglected. They chose Greeks to correct the problem. The group selected seven men. The seven men the group selected, the apostles appointed.

The church grew. Those responsible for the mission of the church didn't leave their chief tasks to do other things. If the apostles had left their work to serve tables, the word couldn't have spread as it did. When elders (parents) do the work of deacons (children), and deacons (children) make policy decisions elders (parents) should make, there'll be unnecessary conflict and stagnation instead of growth. Each member of the body is to function in his or her place.

Acts 6:1-7 is a good example of God's leaders dealing with conflict in a healthy way.

Chapter 31

Preaching During the Interim... Workshops and Closing:
Practical Principles and Closing Sermons

My general practice is to present a workshop once a month on Sunday night.

The workshop rules:

1. They are very practical principles.
2. Workshop is a code-word for I can preach as long as I want to. Some of the lessons last an hour.

Workshops:

*   **How to Accept, Invite, and Enjoy Criticism**. For years I avoided criticism. For that approach, I paid a high price of offense, lack of learning valuable lessons, and eventually, I was told it would be good for me to preach somewhere else. After a session with a counselor one Monday afternoon, I changed my attitude toward criticism. In this workshop, we look at Proverbs about criticism and how to deal with it.

- **We Need More Funerals and Parties.** I use an outline I found on the internet prepared by Tom Miller, a former teacher at East Tennessee School of Preaching and Missions. I'd never preached a sermon on this. I often discussed the concept at leadership workshops. Tom attended one of these workshops shortly after I found the outline. I've preached it often since then.

- **Love Is the Golden Chain that Binds**. One of the most over-used, misused, and abused words in our language is a four-letter word, LOVE. In this workshop, we see the word Jesus commands in our relationship with God, family, each other, and our enemies has no emotion in it. It is a way to treat each other, not a way to feel about others. When understood, it makes a difference in the way we act and feel. It's OK to love someone you don't like.

- **When You Look in the Mirror, Do You Like the Person You See?** How do you see yourself? Are you valuable or worthless? Are you important or unimportant? Are you competent or a klutz? Is there hope for being who God wants you to be?

- **Are You Building Your Life on Facts or Fairy Tales?** Are you looking for the time, place, people, and circumstances where you can live happily ever after? If you had the right job, car, house, spouse, or education, could you live happily ever after?

Two Closing Sermons

- **How Should We Treat the New Preacher?** Throughout my interim, I insert observations about preachers, their needs, and how to be helpful to them. The next-to-last sermon in each church is a lesson on how to treat the new preacher. It's a compilation from many preachers who gave suggestions on how they'd like to be treated—especially when they follow a preacher who has been at a congregation a long time (five or more years). Many people tell me after this sermon they never thought about what I discussed in this lesson.

- **Every Christian Is an Interim Minister.** Many people tell Gail and me they don't see how we go into a congregation, work a few months, leave, and go somewhere else. When you consider it, every Christian is an interim minister. Someone preceded you. Someone(s) will follow you. Your opportunity is to make it easier and better for those who follow.

I preach many more sermons. The past three chapters describe some I think are helpful for transition. As I said at the beginning of the posts on preaching during the interim, I don't think other interim preachers need to preach the same sermons I preach the same way I preach them. This is a report —not a recommendation. I hope you found a "mustard seed" that's been helpful.

Chapter 32
The Search:
Who Will Participate?

It's time to look for the next preacher. Who'll have a part in the search and selection? How will the search be conducted?

Possibilities, Some Ways I've Observed:

1. Recommendation. Contact a favorite preacher, president or head of the Bible department of a Christian college, or the director of a preacher training school and ask for their best recommendation. Take their suggestion. Have the prospect try out. If everything looks OK, offer him the work that night before he accepts an offer from another congregation.

2. "Beauty contest." Assemble a list of many good preachers. Invite them in to speak on successive Sundays. Give members a reply form. Invite the one most members like to be your next preacher unless there were red flags during the interview.

3. Elders serve as the selection group. They decide on a method of search. The elders go ahead with as many candidates as they like, interview, check references, come to a conclusion with or without input from the congregation, and select the new preacher.

4. Elders involve a group(s) to help in the selection process.

I've seen this done three ways:

    a. Begin with a Selection Committee. This group receives résumés, asks for recommendations, makes phone interviews, and presents the Interview Committee with four names. The Interview Committee invites the four men and wives, to come to town for a Friday-Saturday visit for more detailed observation and interviews. An elder meets with this committee to keep the elders informed and up-to-date on the progress and prospect. This group recommends a preacher who comes to meet with the elders. If they find him qualified and a fit, he becomes the next preacher. Another possibility, which I recommend: the pick of the preachers visits with the understanding the congregation will have a voice in the invitation of the elders. I've known of churches who omitted this step and selected a preacher with a shady past. After he comes to the church and repeats past indiscretions, members say, "I could have told you so. But you hired him, and you gave us no opportunity to comment."

    b. Have a Selection Committee who does the tasks of the two committees mentioned above. They narrow the field to four and make recommendations to the elders. The elders invite the four men and wives for their interviews and interaction. They select one man to be considered for the work. That man comes to preach. They ask the congregation to give comments.

c. Have a Selection Committee do all the work, invite the four men, decide on the best man, present him to the congregation, and receive a response from the group after his visit. The elders meet with him during his visit for try-out.

Whatever the method, there should be a clear understanding of the role of each person and group. Develop written descriptions of the authority and expectations of each person in each group about what is and is not expected. Those expectations should be communicated to the congregation. Understand many will not listen, not understand, and forget. That's the reason it needs to be written and repeated over and over during the search process.

Prayer to God for wisdom should precede, saturate, and follow the search for the new preacher.

Chapter 33
Search Team Training:
How Do You Look for a New Preacher?

This is an outline of a training day for the team and elders directly involved in the search process. As always, the wastebasket is available for any ideas that aren't helpful.

Presuppositions:

I believe God loves His church. Jesus built it and died for it (Matthew 16:18; Acts 20:28). God is not only concerned about the church universal but each congregation individually. Several letters of the New Testament are to local groups of believers.

Since God loves His church and wants the best for it, we should invite Him to be part of this process. Remind yourself and others that His wisdom is available to those who pray for it (James 1:5) and work for it (Proverbs 2:1-5).

The process is as important as the product. Christians on the Search and Interview Teams, including the entire eldership, are not just doing a job, but you are participating in an opportunity to grow spiritually. You can learn about God, about others, and about yourself.

Each committee should become a group before they see the first résumé or mention the first preacher's name. A friend used to say, "I dream of a place and a time where Christians can get together and tell the truth." The interview and selection process should be one of those times and places.

If one holds back, does not speak his mind, doesn't ask important questions, doesn't add helpful insight, or is in any way intimidated or compromised, the group and the church is deprived of group wisdom. Becoming a group will require several meetings before they "get on with the Lord's work" of selecting a preacher. I believe learning to get along with each other, discussing how we're going to conduct business, including how we'll settle conflict when it arises, and getting to know each other in order to "stir up love and good works" is part of "the Lord's work."

The training day is designed to begin this process. It's only the beginning. Usually, a group goes through three stages before it is ready to function:

1. Forming.
2. Storming.
3. Norming.

I include activities in the training to begin those stages. I conducted these training sessions on a Saturday.

7:30   Breakfast. We start with a light meal. Eating together begins the group process. Many things happen when we are eating to bring us together.

After breakfast, I get the group into a circle. Everyone is facing everyone else. Everyone is on the front row.

Prayer is a part of our day at many different times. We pray for wisdom. We pray for the members of the search and interview team. We pray for the elders. We pray for the next preacher. We pray for the men who will be considered who will want to come but will not be selected. We pray for this church and the body of Christ over the world.

8:00   Guidelines. I begin any group (counseling session, Bible class, Family Meeting, Stress Session in a monthly ministers' workshop) with negotiating guidelines. Family (group) rules are usually unconscious, unspoken, understood, and contradictory. That makes for difficult communication. I want the rules to be spoken, conscious, understood, and as productive we we can make it. These are the boundaries that improve the possibility that "Christians can get together and tell the truth." "Can two walk together, unless they are agreed" (Amos 3:3)? The answer to that question is, "No!" Many discussions end in chaos or miscommunication because we didn't talk about how we were going to talk. Check Guidelines for a Good Discussion in Chapter 21.

8:35   Mixer, introduction. The people line up according to birthdays: January – December. They get into pairs. Each person interviews the other, preparing to introduce the partner to the group. Tell something about yourself and include something that no one knows about you until today. Each person introduces his/her partner.

8:45   What do you bring to this process? It is interesting how different people contribute to the search process. Some are good at calling, recording, leading the meetings, writing letters or emails, asking interview questions, arranging for visits to the congregation, keeping spreadsheets of where each candidate is in the process, preparing sermons on CDs or MP3s for others to hear. We learn more about that in this section of the training session.

9:15   What will you get out of this? Each person needs to examine his motives. "Keep your heart with all diligence, for out of it spring the issues of life" (Proverbs 4:23). The search process is long and sometimes difficult and frustrating. Unless there is adequate motivation, the members will get discouraged. That can result in some people quitting or rushing the process to "get it over with" and the process will end with less than excellent results.

Break

9:45   Anytown Church now—10 years from now. After the break, I bring people to tables with crayons and large drawing paper. I ask each person to draw a line vertically in the middle of the page. On the left side of the paper, each person draws his or her impression of this congregation now. On the right side of the page, each person draws his or her hopes and dreams for this church ten years from now. After everyone is finished, we come back into the circle and discuss the pictures. Everyone is learning what others see now and what they want to see in the future. These ideas will help form what they want to see in the next preacher.

10:30   Reading "mustard seeds". A few weeks before, I have given everyone a book on the selection process. During this session, each person shares some ideas gained that may be helpful in selecting the next preacher for this congregation. Some suggested books for preacher search . My recommended books are *The Search Committee Handbook: The Step-by-Step Guide to Hiring Your Next Minister*, by Don Viar, and *When to Leave...Before You Go*, by Wade Hodges.

11:15   Search Committee, Interview Committee, Elders. This is where we discuss the job description of each committee and the elders. It is necessary to have a clear understanding of what each group is and is not to do in the process.

12:00   Lunch.

12:45   Chain Letter. After lunch, I read a chain letter about preachers. See "Preacher Chain Letter" in the Appendix.

1:00   Preacher of your dreams—preacher of your nightmares. It's back to the drawing paper and crayons for this exercise. As before, I ask each person to draw a line down the middle of the paper. On the left side, please draw a representation of the "Preacher of Your Dreams." If you could get the perfect preacher, what would he look like? What's the kind of preacher you want for this congregation? This will certainly include something about his stand for truth but also attitudes, mannerisms, and personality—both in and out of the pulpit. What should be his emphasis? In what areas would you tolerate weaknesses in order to have strengths in other areas?

After everyone is finished with that, on the right side of the paper, please draw the "Preacher of Your Nightmares." What would the opposite of the "Preacher of Your Dreams" look like?

When all are finished, we get into the circle to discuss these works of art and visualizations of our expectations of the next preacher. I allow each one to tell about his/her picture and his/her preacher.

My final question in this exercise is, "What if the preacher of your dreams is someone else's nightmare?" How will you work with others who have different expectations of the next preacher? That is the challenge of the selection committee—whether it is the elders doing the whole process or whether a group makes recommendations to the elders for their consideration before making the decision. Will each person listen to the other and will everyone express their thoughts and feelings freely to contribute to the final selection?

1:30 Suggestions for Preacher Search is a collection of my thoughts and observations as I have experienced and watched this process. I express my best judgment. As always, the wastebasket is available for anything not worth taking home.

1:45 Evaluation. A good way for me to learn is to do the best I know how and ask others to help me improve. In evaluating the training session, I ask two questions?
- What did you learn?
- How can this training be better next time?

We conclude at 2:00 with a prayer for God to bless the process and bless us to take advantage of this opportunity to grow in our faith in God, connection to each other, and improvement in our wisdom, skills, and attitude.

Chapter 34
Preacher Search — Interviews:
What Will You Ask and What Will You Be Asked?

The search team has read recommendations and résumés. They've sorted their first impressions into A, B, and C categories. It's time to continue the evaluation.

The search team and prospective preacher should consider, compile, and practice two sets of questions:

1. What will I ask?
2. What will I be asked?

If I'm concerned with only one side of the interview, what I want to know, I'll be half-prepared. That will come across when the other party begins to ask questions. I need to prepare a repertoire of responses to every question I may be asked by the other person(s).

Presuppositions:

- **The purpose of the interview isn't to "get the job" or "hire this good preacher."** The purpose of interview-evaluation is to see if we fit. There are many good preachers and many good congregations that don't need to be together. They don't fit. They may be equally righteous and faithful. But they don't fit. There are many good men and good women that don't need to be married. They are good Christians following Jesus. But they don't fit each other.

- **Each of the interviewing parties should be equally eager to give and receive critical information that will help the other make a good decision.**

- **Both the church and preacher are trying out.** Both have choices. Either can reject the other. If one wants to work together and the other doesn't, they don't fit. It takes two to make a match. It takes one to reject an offer.

- **The best time to get a divorce is before you get married.** If there's anything that would be a disappointment and deal breaker, it's better to find out during the interview than six months after the new preacher has moved and someone is surprised — the church or the preacher.

- **Faith grows through creative doubt** (Mark 9:23, 24). Ask what you need to know and check with independent sources to substantiate or question answers during the interview. I plan to discuss this further in Checking References.

- **An excellent principle during the search process:**

   Therefore, whatever you want men to do to you, do also to them, for this is the Law and the Prophets (Matthew 7:12).

Interviews
Church to Preacher

The general principle: ask what you need to know to make a good selection of the preacher and the church. Ask enough to discover what you like about the other, what you don't like, and whether you can put up with what you don't like to enjoy what you like.

Look in the Appendix for samples of the following tools I have collected from friends and churches where I've worked.

1. Phone Interview.
2. Pulpit Minister Interview Questions.
3. Minister Interview Summary.
4. Letter to Applicant.
5. Letter of Regret.

In addition to these questions, I suggest:

- **Discuss media involvement on Facebook, Twitter, other media.** Exchange friendship, follows, and check the past year of posts.

- **Discuss how the preacher deals with political issues, your philosophy of the Christian and government, and how it should be handled from the pulpit, in classes, bulletin, and on social media.**

- **Ask about sermon preparation.** What percentage of your sermons come from preparation from scratch, what percent from reworked sermons of lessons heard on the internet, lectureships, etc., and what percent copies from internet sources such as Sermon Central.

- **Ask about previous involvement in pornography in print, on the internet, movies, or other sources, and how he guards against this.** This is a problem for many ministers, as well as other Christians. If you decide this is unimportant, be prepared to deal with an angry, depressed preacher who will have to be right on every issue, or who'll have to change everything his way to grow and please the Lord, and could act out sexual issues with members of the congregation. To prepare for this question, practice with all members of the Search Team and elders in case the preacher prospect is interested in the same issue with you (Matthew 7:12).

You may find these questions inadequate for your needs. Delete the questions you think are unnecessary, add questions you think are vital, and you'll have an ideal list for your search.

I suggest a practice session before your first interview. I did this with one interim congregation. I was the preaching candidate. They asked me their questions. I answered. I asked questions a preacher might ask.

Preacher to Church

If you're on the Search Team or if you are an elder interviewing a prospective preacher, what will he ask you?

You can read questions by three preachers in the Appendix.
1. Dale Jenkins.
2. Bryan McAlister.
3. Jeremy Houck.

You may find these inadequate for your needs. They ask the wrong questions. They don't ask the right questions. Delete the unnecessary questions, add vital questions, and you'll have an ideal list for your search.

Chapter 35
Checking References:
Do You Want to Know the Truth?

———————————

"Everything looks good. This man is impressive. He's devoted to Jesus. His sermons on the net are outstanding—Biblical, interesting, challenging, authentic, and applicable to daily life. His wife and family seem to be dedicated and a compliment to the preacher's ministry. His interview was outstanding! He answered questions well. His questions were relevant and challenging for the search group. I say let's offer him the work before someone else gets him!"

What about checking references?

"What else could you want? He preaches, lives, and applies God's word. He was recommended by a friend of mine who said he didn't know anything against him. We better call quickly or he'll be gone."

Checking references is often a distraction in the process. Many people who call me as a reference for a preacher come across as someone who wants me to confirm the decision they've already made to secure this man.

It's the responsibility of the search team to find a disciple of Jesus who is a competent, caring, and clean man who will be the next preacher. To do that, the searchers need to do due diligence to find the truth which will set them, the preacher, and the congregation free to enter into a good relationship.

There's no problem in securing the "chief of sinners" to be the next preacher if he's received mercy, has put off the old man, and is continually putting on the new man. It's a problem if the old man is denied, still lives in the back bedroom, and visits in his life frequently.

If the preacher has no issues with most forms of immorality, but is lazy, filled with uncontrolled anger, incompetent, dull, or uncooperative, the best time to learn about any of these things is before he loads up the U-Haul coming your way.

What do you ask a reference?

You need to address many aspects of the prospective preacher's life to contribute to a good fit for the ministry you want in your congregation. The best material I've seen came from the *Minister Transition Packet*, prepared by Dr. Charles Siburt. I bought a copy several years ago. It's full of good ideas about the transition process. They now have different packets for securing preachers, youth ministers, and for ministers looking. Go on the web to Abilene Christian University,

Minister Transition Resources. It has many tools for the transition.

I will be glad to send you the reference form I've modified for search teams. I have it in .doc and PDF formats: *jerrie@barberclippings.com.*

Call the reference to make an appointment to do the interview. I plan on forty-five minutes to an hour. I prefer a personal meeting, but often it isn't practical.

I like to go over the rules: why I'm calling, confidentiality for the person answering questions, the importance of providing information, and our desire to do what's best for the preacher, his family, the church where he's working now, and our congregation. I want to know his strengths and weaknesses. If a reference doesn't give any weaknesses, I disregard that contact. Either he or she doesn't know the person well enough or isn't being forthright with the information.

A church isn't ready to invite a preacher to work with them until they know what they like, what they don't like, and how they plan to put up with what they don't like. A preacher isn't ready to move to a church until he knows what he likes, at least a thing or two he won't like, and how he plans to put up with what he doesn't like.

In addition to a thorough checking of references—both the ones submitted by the candidate and more references suggested by initial references, you should:

- **Do a criminal background check.**
- **Do a credit check.**
- **Discuss with the preacher any unfavorable reports you received.** Determine any truth which will set you free to proceed or stop the process with this person (Matthew 7:12).

Check laws in your state about proper permission to do a criminal background check and credit check. You may need to get written permission to do these.

I don't know how to over-emphasize the necessity of working hard to know the person you're considering to work with you and your people in the intimate and essential areas of life, death, sin, holiness, family, discipleship, loving God, and our neighbors. Regardless of his eloquence and pizzazz, if his life doesn't back up his message, he isn't the man for your pulpit.

Chapter 36

Suggestions for the Preacher Search:
Suggestions From Observation and Experience About Looking for a Preacher

---

This started as a hand-out during the training workshop for the group looking for and evaluating the next preacher. These are things I've learned from the University of Hard Knocks. Consider what I say and feel free to use the wastebasket.

• **Invite God to be part of this process.** Remind yourself and others that His wisdom is available to those who pray for it (James 1:5) and work for it (Proverbs 2:1-5). You're starting a lengthy, difficult, invigorating, enlightening, and frustrating journey. Neither you individually nor the group collectively has the wisdom to deal with all issues, individuals, families, and churches you'll be affecting as you carry out your task. Each person, including yourself, is a creation of God deserving to be treated with respect and love. God's word gives us principles for every situation in life. God promised to give us wisdom when we realize we don't have it. I suggest you begin this search being poor in spirit and begging God for wisdom you need.

• **The process is as important as the product.** Christians on the Search/Interview committees are not just doing a job. You are participating in an opportunity to grow spiritually. You can learn about God, others, and yourself. Be aware of your hopes, fears, prejudices, and faith. Watch for growth. Thank God for the opportunity to take part in this good work and the strength and wisdom He furnishes.

• **What are your rules?** What are the spoken guidelines? What are the unspoken expectations? Don't start talking until you agree, as a group, how you're going to talk. Some suggested guidelines: Discussion Rules, Chapter 21. Good agreements reduce conflict before conflict begins. If you don't have conflict —differences of opinion—several of you are unnecessary. The reason we have a committee instead of a CEO, is to get different perspectives. The goal is to create an atmosphere where each person feels free and is encouraged to express every viewpoint. What may seem trivial to you, may spark an idea in another person and will make a difference in the outcome.

• **Spend five minutes at the end of each session to evaluate the process.** How did we do? Was I heard? How am I feeling about what we're doing? How am I relating to others in the group? Do I feel part of the team? It's easy for a dominant personality or two to monopolize and unduly influence the group. Many people won't talk unless they're asked. Be concerned. Be honest. Be interested in the best choice possible. The chairman should ask each person about the process and how they feel about how they interacted during the meeting today.

• **Consider a "no suicide" contract for the search team.** Sometimes people get tired, disillusioned, or frustrated when working on a project. They may quit unexpectedly in disgust: "Now they'll know how important I was." A better way is to keep current. It may be during selection that one or more will have a good reason not to complete the assignment. Communicate to the group your intentions and reasons and give them time to adjust to your absence on the committee. Rule 1 is to let God be a part of the process. It's not Christian conduct to ignore the teaching of Jesus when you're searching for a preacher—or any other time. Considerate family members don't disappear and never explain where they went and why they didn't show up when expected.

• **When you're pursuing a "good preacher," your first task is not to "hire" him.** The first goal is to help you and him decide if this church is a good fit for him and you. When and if you talk with a "good preacher," and you or he decides it's not a good fit, you've been more successful than if you'd "hired" a "good preacher" that didn't fit.

Some good eligible men don't need to marry some good eligible women—not because either is bad or unChristian. They just don't fit. Many good preachers don't need to be preaching in many good congregations—not because they're bad preachers or the churches are bad churches. They're good. But they don't fit. From my perspective, this is one of the first tasks of the search team and prospective preacher—determine if you fit. If you don't fit, you're wasting time talking about salary, insurance, vacation, number of weeks off for meetings, workshops, and lectureships, retirement plans, and whether to rent a U-Haul or call North American Van Lines.

• **Remember it's not only the preacher that's "trying out."** The congregation is also "trying out." Both have choices. If he's a "good preacher," he's watching and investigating every aspect of this congregation just as you're watching and investigating him.

Our family served as Shoney's and Captain D's mystery shoppers for six years. We ate at the restaurants once a week and filled out a form, answering questions to check the restaurant, staff, and food each week. As soon as we ate, we mailed the form to their headquarters to help them know how they were doing. They took our suggestions and made adjustments.

When we moved the next time, we made a Shoney's Mystery Shopper form for each church where we were "trying out." The church was "trying out" from the first contact until we completed our decision where we were moving.

In the Appendix, there are samples of notes I made during one move in my ministry.

At one church where I served as an interim, they narrowed their search to four men. They invited each of them and his wife to visit on successive Friday-Saturdays. They interviewed, showed the community, and continued their evaluation of each other.

On one weekend, the preacher stayed over on Saturday night and visited Bible classes and worship the next morning. I wasn't aware of this, and very few in the congregation knew— just the search team who saw him. I asked the congregation the next Sunday if they were aware they were "trying out" the previous Sunday. I told them one of the four top preacher candidates was present. He was watching and listening, observing singing, praying, friendliness or unfriendliness, the condition of the building and grounds, and getting on-site impressions of what kind of church this was and whether there was a fit. Often search teams go to a prospective preacher's congregation, observing him. It's also valuable for a preacher to do this. I call this "equalizing the pressure."

• **Don't promise prospective preachers much.** Each member of the search team should be careful not to discuss your preferences and give an indication to a preacher he's the "top pick" when the group hasn't reached a decision.

Avoid feel-good phrases without specific meaning, "We'll take care of you when you get here."

Think before you promise, "We'll call you Tuesday night at 7:00 p.m."

• **Do what you promise.** One of the most disappointing things in my years of ministry is a failure of elders and search committees to call when they promised. Often an interview would end with the statement, "We'll meet and discuss this. We'll call you Tuesday night at 7:00 p.m. to let you know what we decided."

My question, "Central time or Eastern time?" When clarified, I wrote the telephone appointment in my DayTimer™.

As Tuesday night approached, I told my children, "I have an important call Tuesday night at 8:00 p.m. If one of your friends calls from 7:45 on, tell them, 'Daddy has an important call coming at 8:00. I'll call you back.'"

8:00 came and went; 8:15, 8:30, 9:00. No call. My reasoning: elders usually meet on Wednesday night. That's what they probably meant. They'll call after services. On the way home from Bible study, the conversation with my children, "I may have an important call coming in tonight. If one of your friends calls, tell them, 'Daddy is expecting an important call. I'll call you back later.'"

No call on Wednesday, Thursday — often never. I'd learn about their new preacher when I read an announcement in the *Gospel Advocate*. This happened time after time.

This practice was so pronounced that one elder who did what he promised stands out. In 1988, I learned at Freed-Hardeman lectures the church in Amory, Mississippi, was looking for a preacher. I called one of the elders, Jimmy Vaughan, and talked with him. He told me, "Yes, we're looking. We heard you might be available. We may want to talk with you. We're talking with one man at a time. We're talking with a preacher now, and it looks like we may come to an agreement. If we don't, we want to talk with you next. We plan to decide this weekend. I'll call you Tuesday night at 7:00 p.m. and let you know, either way."

"Central time or Eastern time?"

"Central time."

My conversation with my children, "I have an important call Tuesday night at 8:00 p.m. If one of your friends calls from 7:45 on, tell them, 'Daddy has an important call coming at 8:00. I'll call you back.' "

Tuesday night came. I was waiting. At 8:00 p.m., 7:00 CST, my phone rang in Dalton, Georgia.

"This is Jimmy Vaughan from Amory, Mississippi." That's when he said he would call!

From that day, every time I saw Jimmy Vaughan, I would address him, "There's Jimmy Vaughan from Amory, Mississippi, the elder who tells the truth." In notes in my Contacts list on my iPhone under Jimmy Vaughan, I have this written, "the elder who tells the truth" - 1988. In notes below Contacts information in his daughter's entry, "Daughter of Jimmy Vaughn, Amory, Mississippi, the elder who tells the truth."

I've labored this point because in my experience, and in the experience of many preachers who've talked with me, this practice is common. That should not be!

During the time of looking for a preacher isn't the time to disregard principles or Biblical morality of telling the truth and being considerate of others.

• **Keep everyone in the process informed.** Considering moving is a time of stress for many people: the preacher, his wife, his children, the congregation where he's working, if they know about his consideration, and other congregations he's considering. If a person is no longer in consideration, let him know. If it'll be longer to complete a particular phase than you stated, let the people involved know. If it's been some time since you communicated to those involved and you don't have anything to say, let them know you don't have anything to say.

Both preachers and churches should study verbal and non-verbal communication. We're beginning to tell each other how we'll treat each other when we get together.

• **Be sensitive to the family.** The wife and children will be part of the decision and will be vital to the happiness after the move. A special activity for the children when they visit will impress. Leaving them in a motel to watch TV while Dad is being interviewed will also leave an impression.

When the family visits to begin making the final decision, continue to plan activities to give them information about the church and community, but also leave adequate free time. They need time to pray, talk about you, question, doubt, make calls for advice, and think.

• **Plan a Funeral—Graduation Party at the conclusion to celebrate your good work and to reflect on what you have learned about God, about His church, about others, and about yourself.**

My policy for being a reference at an interim congregation is included in my last paragraph of this training document, "Suggestions for the Preacher Search:"

> I appreciate your willingness to work on this significant task. I've enjoyed our time together. I'm glad to give thoughts on looking for a preacher. I won't discuss the persons you consider. I won't be a reference for or a critic against men who apply.

May God bless you as you seek His wisdom in this process.

Chapter 37

When and How Will the Next Preacher Leave?
How Long Do You Plan to Stay? How Do You Plan to Leave?

What's something you need to discuss with your prospective preacher before you sign the job description and contract? I think there needs to be a clear understanding: how long do you plan to stay and how do you plan to leave?

This Needs To Be Discussed For The Benefit Of The Church: How Long Do You Plan to Stay?

Growing churches have preachers that stay a long time. Preachers staying a long time doesn't guarantee church growth. But I've never seen or heard of a growing church changing preachers every two to five years.

If a preacher's making this move as a stepping stone to a larger congregation or if he's taking this opportunity to hold him until a church opens up in a more desirable location, it may not be wise to choose him as your next preacher.

How Do You Plan to Leave?

A preacher can destroy his previous ministry and damage the congregation if he leaves with a bad attitude.

He can make the transition easy when he cooperates with his departure, regardless of the reason. It's easy to think elders are wise when they want us to come and decide they lose their wisdom when they ask us to leave.

This Needs to Be Discussed for the Benefit of the Preacher: What Would it Take for You to Ask Me to Leave and How Will You Treat My Family and Me Should That Happen?

Some churches have a plan to change preachers on a regular basis. I talked with one preacher who'd been at a congregation for four and a half years. The church was growing. The congregation seemed to be happy. The preacher and his family were enjoying their work. The elders informed him it was time for him to be looking for another congregation.

"What's wrong?" the surprised preacher asked.

"Nothing's wrong," the elders answered. "We have a policy we change preachers every five years. You've been here four and a half years, and we want to give you plenty of time to find another church."

The best time to plan a funeral is before a terminal illness. It's easier to select caskets, clothes, a preacher for the funeral, pallbearers, songs, and other special requests when everyone is well and happy.

The best time to discuss how dismissal might be conducted is when elders think they're selecting the best preacher in the brotherhood and the preacher thinks he's found the perfect church. There's no conflict then. Emotions are pleasant. Everyone's happy. Let's talk about a possible head-on collision no one saw coming and decide how we'll treat each other if the tragedy occurs.

Elders' Preparation for This Discussion

The best way for elders to prepare for this discussion, is to have the same understanding about their tenure and departure. One of the most destructive things that can happen in a church is have a "leadership suicide."

"I hereby resign as a...of this congregation—effective immediately!" There may be a nod of the head, his wife rises, and they exit the back door. Or a gasp, when even his wife didn't know it was coming. I've observed or heard of it happening from elders, deacons, and preachers. Without discussion or planning, an angry or discouraged leader may express his frustration by leaving without warning.

When elders have an understanding in place, they introduce this discussion by telling the prospective preacher, "This is the way we operate. We have a 'no-suicide' agreement in our eldership and with our deacons. We believe smooth transitions are important in any group and especially in the Lord's church. Let's discuss your leaving when we're excited about your coming. Our commitment to you: we'll follow Jesus' teaching to treat you as we want others to treat us."

It would be good to continue to have this discussion during each annual review. Providing financial incentives and checking to be sure the preacher is preparing for eventual leaving by elders' request, choice, retirement, disability, or death is a kindness shown by caring shepherds. It's better to have hard conversations when they're easy!

Chapter 38
The Preacher Who Is Being Considered - 1:
How Were You Approached?

"What's the least amount of money it'd take for us to get'cha to come and be our preacher?" This conversation was the first contact with this church—the worst approach I've ever received inviting me to consider working with another church.

Elders and search committees tell much in the first contact. Are you interested in just some preacher or me? What have you learned about me that makes you think we might be compatible and I would be effective where you are? What will be your selection process? I'm not interested in a "beauty contest"—asking ten to twelve preachers to come in successive Sundays, select the best sermon, and invite him to be your next preacher. I've participated in that when I was desperate. It's better not to be desperate. Let me share with you a welcomed contrast to that approach.

The Best Approach I've Ever Experienced or Heard:
• **On June 4, 1984, I received a call from a man.** He said he and another man wanted to talk with me 25-30 minutes. He was in

Montgomery, Alabama. They would be in Dalton, Georgia, at 4:00. When they arrived, they introduced themselves as two elders from a church in Texas. They were looking for a preacher. They had an impressive introductory packet of information about the church. They wanted me to read it, and they would get back to me. I told them I wasn't interested in moving to Texas. They replied, "We aren't asking you to move to Texas. We want you to read the information, and we'll talk to you later." I told my elders Wednesday night about their visit and my response.

• **In about two weeks, they called requesting me to answer some questions to see if we were compatible.** I told them I wasn't interested in moving to Texas. One of the elders said, "I'm not asking you to move to Texas. The elders would like to know more about you, what you believe, and how you work. It may be we wouldn't fit." They were the same questions they asked prospective members and which they used to evaluate Bible class teachers. I told my elders about the questionnaire.

• **In another two weeks, I received a call, requesting my family and me to visit the church and community.** They wanted us to see the area, meet the other elders, and talk some more. We flew out on Thursday and returned on Saturday. They wanted to arrange another visit. I told them I wasn't interested in moving to Texas. The only way I'd return was with a consultant from Atlanta, Georgia. He was a marriage and family therapist and a consultant with churches. I said, "It isn't fair how we interview and hire preachers. There's eight of you and one of me. When one of you is talking, seven of you are thinking. When I'm talking, nobody's thinking. I need help. Coming here would be a major move for my family and me." I told my elders in Dalton before and after I went.

• **In about two weeks, they called and said they were ready for my counselor and me to come.** We spent seven hours talking with the staff and eight hours talking with the elders. The elders and my counselor had an hour without me. I discussed this trip with my elders in Dalton.

We had an understanding I would have two or three days to think if they invited me to work with them. My family and I discussed it. On Labor Day, I called and told them I had decided to stay in Dalton and thanked them for one of the most challenging and growing experiences of my ministry. It was the best deliberation process I've ever known.

The following Wednesday night, I talked with my elders at Central in Dalton. I knew many in the congregation had heard about our talking with the other church in Texas. I told them if I'd damaged my relationship with the church, I'd resign and begin looking for another congregation. After discussing this, they told me they wanted me to stay. We had another four years of good ministry in Dalton.

Observations about the Process

1. We took the time we needed to think. Often a church invites a preacher in for a Sunday. He teaches Sunday morning Bible class and preaches Sunday morning and Sunday night. He and the elders meet an hour before Sunday night services. Then they make a decision affecting the church, the preacher, and his family for years to come. We involved three months from the first contact to the final decision.

2. They were willing to invest time, effort, and money to make a good choice. The brethren at the church in Texas had the names of several preachers. They visited each one, delivering information for each to consider. That was a long missionary journey from Texas, to Montgomery, Alabama, to Dalton, Georgia, and perhaps other places. They thought it was important.

3. As the summer progressed, I had the idea they were interested in me—not just "a preacher," and I would be fortunate if they chose me.

4. They and I were willing to ask questions and make statements to get to the issue of whether this move was good

for their church and my family and me. We talked about what we liked and didn't like. We expressed what was impressive and how we were disappointed.

5. We used outside help. They had a counselor in the congregation who participated and observed many of our discussions. My counselor was helpful to them and me. He and I talked between sessions. He observed the discussions. He suggested questions and areas needing more exploration. My family met with him several times during the summer.

6. The elders at the church in Texas told me the summer was helpful to them and gave them wisdom in selecting their next preacher. This process should involve more than a weekend.

A church selecting a preacher and a preacher selecting a church is more important than, "Where would you like to eat tonight?". The time, thought, effort, research, and prayer should demonstrate that.

Chapter 39
The Preacher Who Is Being Considered - 2:
Are They Interested in You...or Just Anybody?

The goal of the church looking for a preacher isn't to hire a preacher. It's to find a fit to mutually bless the church and the preacher. The goal of the preacher looking for a church isn't to find the first church who'll let him move. It's to find a church where they and he can grow together.

There are many good Christian single men who don't need to marry any one of many good Christian single women. It isn't because either is sinful or bad. They don't fit.

There are many good, faithful, and effective gospel preachers who don't need to work with many good, faithful, and effective congregations. It isn't because they're bad, liberals, or legalists. They just don't fit.

There are many reasons why there may not be a fit: language, culture, background, education, economics, or interests. A man who is accepted and loved in one church may be rejected or ignored in another.

How Is the Church Going about Their Search?

- **How have they followed up with you?** Have they called when they said they would?

- **Do they communicate they'll be fortunate if you decide to work with them?** Yes, you should be talking with a church where you feel you'll be fortunate to work with them. "Let nothing be done through selfish ambition or conceit, but in lowliness of mind let each esteem others better than himself" (Philippians 2:3).

- **How many other people are they talking to?** Are you one of ten or twelve? Will they invite a person to work with them who the most people want at the end of three months and ten tryouts?

- **What kind of questions are they asking?** I went to one church who asked two questions, "Do you believe a person has to be baptized to go to heaven?" and "Are you anti?".

- **What are they learning about you personally?** You need to be compatible doctrinally. You also need to match the preacher-elder relationship each of you want. Will they accept you as a participant in elders' meetings or will you work with little interaction and if you do anything wrong, they'll let you know?

- **How much do they know about your family and how concerned are they about them and their happiness in this church and this community?**

- **What kind of research have they done or do they plan to do before they make their decision?** Have they checked references? When I ask a person to serve as a reference, I ask them to let me know when the church contacts them. I want to know if they're doing their homework. Have they or will they do a criminal background check and credit check? Will they check to confirm you went to schools listed on your résumé and received certificates or degrees you stated?

- **How do you and they see you fitting into their work?** Do they see you as someone who will help them do what they're already doing? Do they expect you to change many things to make the church grow? Will you be responsible for the church growing?

- **Are they looking for a preacher just like the one they had?**

- **Are they looking for a preacher opposite of the one they had?**

- **Have they been cooperative and encourage you to say what you need to say and ask what you need to ask?** Or, did they set aside one hour before the evening service for the entire interview?

- **How much time are they willing to take to assure this is helpful to everyone involved?** The time they are taking now indicates how much mutual effort you can expect to build enriching relationships and God-glorifying work.

- **What and how did they pay you for your interview and try-out?** That is one of the non-verbal communications of how you will be treated financially after you arrive.

Chapter 40
The Preacher Who Is Being Considered - 3:
Are You Interested in This Church or Just Anywhere?

_____

The easiest time to move is when you don't want to and don't have to. If you're not running away from something, it's easier to go somewhere better. I've tried it both ways. There's a difference in either being fired or resigning with nowhere to go with a time limit and being pursued by a church when you're secure and don't have to move. But in either situation, it's good to remember that going where you don't fit is an opportunity to be doing the same thing in a short time.

Some Questions To Check Your Fit with this Church
1. Why do the elders think you might be a person who will work well with this congregation?

2. How did the way you've been doing ministry lead them to you?

3. How will the leadership style of the elders fit your preference of a working relationship?

4. How often will you be meeting, talking, and planning with the elders on the direction and growth of this congregation?

5. How does your education and interests fit the church you're considering? A man with a PhD who plays polo might have to count those as loss if he plans to work with people who have a high school education, or less, and whose main interest is coon hunting.

6. What are you learning about the community? Will you be doing cross-cultural ministry? If you grew up in New York city, moving to a small community in Tennessee or Alabama without a Walmart may be difficult for you, your wife, and children.

7. How will your wife and children fit into this church and community?

8. What are their expectations for you besides preaching? Are you willing and excited about those ministry opportunities?

9. What do you and your family need for education, recreation, and medical care and do you find those in this community?

10. What are your goals for ministry in other areas such as workshops, revivals, teaching and attending seminars and lectureships? Will you be encouraged in these?

11. How much of what they desire in their next preacher is the result of a reaction to what they didn't like in their last preacher?

12. Are they trying to reproduce the perfect preacher who just left for another church after serving them for twenty years?

13. How much of what you're looking for in your next church is a result of what is upsetting in the church where you're working now?

14. Are you running from a person or small group of people who torment you where you are? Are you aware those kinds of people already live in any church where you'll be moving? You probably have them in your family as well. When you work out your family issues, the church people won't bother you as much.

15. Have you learned what you don't like as well as what you like? How are you going to put up with what you don't like? Are you willing to put up with it for twenty years?

Are you running away from something or are you going somewhere?

Chapter 41
The Preacher Who Is Being Considered – 4:
Have You Checked the Church's References?

The preacher may feel intense pressure during the interview, with the search committee or elders being completely relaxed. If that's true, it's unfortunate. Everybody's trying out. The church has choices. There're many preachers available to move. The preacher has choices. There are many churches looking for preachers. The more everyone realizes and understands, the better the selection can go.

It was next to the last move I'd make as a full-time preacher. A former college classmate, now serving as an elder, called: "I hear you might consider moving."

"Yes, I'm looking."
"Would you consider moving to Mobile, Alabama?"
"I'm open now to anywhere in the lower forty-eight states."

"Good. Send me a résumé, three tapes (remember those and rewinding?), and three references and we'll look at them."

"I'll get those in the mail tomorrow. Please send me your attendance and contribution numbers for the past five years, three tapes of your present preacher's Sunday morning and Sunday night sermons, and three references."

"...why do you want those?"
"Why do you want my information?"
"We don't know you."
"I don't know you. Why don't we start getting acquainted."

My friend seemed surprised that I'd ask for anything. I was as interested in learning about the congregation as they were concerned about me.

Eleven years earlier, when I was moving, I developed a list of questions I discussed with elders during my interviews. Often, they'd ask if I had any questions. When I pulled the pages of questions out, they seemed relieved. That gave us something to talk about. I was trying to solve every doctrinal and procedural issue. If I could get the right match with all these, we wouldn't have problems while I preached there. It didn't work that way.

Sixteen years after compiling the first list, I wrote another list. These questions would be the basis of my interviews with:
- Preachers for the past twenty-five years.
- Associates, youth ministers.
- Custodians.

- Happy members.
- Unhappy members.
- Members who left happy.
- Members who left unhappy.

See the Appendix for questions I ask: Preacher Interview, Staff Interview.

Notice my emphasis in these questions: is this church aware of its strengths and weaknesses and do they and I want to work together to grow to be more like Jesus wants His people to be?

I've found one of the most productive questions to ask is: "Matthew 7:12 - If I were in your place and you were in mine, what would you want me to tell you?" When I've been quiet and listened, I've often received valuable information.

Chapter 42
Leaving an Interim Church:
Finishing and Saying Goodbye

Someone, in one of our interim congregations, asked Gail, "Doesn't it hurt when you have to leave a church after getting to know people and making new friends?"

Gail's reply was, "Yes, it hurts."

"Then why do you do it?"

"Would it be better to get to know you, have friends for life, and hurt leaving, or never to have known you?"

The metaphor that makes sense to me is serving as foster parents. When a family takes a foster child, they know they'll give up the child when their home is ready to reenter or when they're adopted. The family will miss the child. But they're doing a valuable service caring for this child during transition.

Some preachers and other humans don't like to say goodbye. It's uncomfortable. It hurts.

Life is hard. That's part of the challenge of transition. People don't want to hurt. They want to get comfortable quickly. Therefore, they want to:

1. Get it back like it was.
2. Hurry and get through this so we can get back to the Lord's work, not realizing walking through the valley of the shadow of death is part of the Lord's work.

I make a conscious effort to finish, get ready for the next preacher (which I've been doing since I started this interim), and say goodbye. That's one of the advantages of the interim relationship. What I do is in no way trying to keep my job; I've already quit. I'm not trying to get a raise; I don't stay long enough to get a raise. I have a limited time. I have a few opportunities to make a difference, as every person in every situation — limited time and few opportunities.

I enjoy connecting with all age groups. I begin playing with children the first day I arrive. We exchange high-fives. I tell them they are POWERFUL! I don't want to not show up one Sunday with my absence being the first indication to the children I'm leaving.

About a month before we finish, when we know our departure date, I ask parents to start talking with their children about us leaving. As the time approaches, I talk to them, to their ability to understand, about us not seeing them each week. I invite them to come to see us at our new location or in Nashville when we're there. Gail and I were thrilled a few weeks ago when a family from Northside in Jeffersonville, Indiana, showed up at our front door to visit. People become important to us, and it's good to keep in touch.

Once we have a departure day, either when the new preacher comes or the end of our commitment, I begin saying goodbye. My model is something I read years ago:

The Five Acts of Dying

1. **Forgive me.** If I've been hurtful or negligent in any way, I want to correct it before I leave.

2. **I forgive you.** If any relationships need repairing, I want to finish before I leave.

3. **Thank you.** Gratitude is good for the giver and the recipient. It's easy to find occasions of graciousness to recognize and express appreciation.

4. **I love you.** We're not leaving because we don't love you or like you. We're leaving because this is what we do. We're rendering a service. We've enjoyed and have been blessed by our time with you. We go to another church to bless and be blessed by them.

5. **Goodbye.** I don't use euphemisms such as, "It's not goodbye, but so long. It'll still be the same as when we were here. We'll be back often." That isn't accurate. It won't be the same. We won't be back often. We're working with our eighth interim church. We don't have time to visit previous places often. It's goodbye.

I promise to stay away for a year. Even when we've been close to Nashville or our new interim, we don't drop in on our immediate past interims. The new preacher and his family need to get acquainted with the church without our interruption.

I schedule a visit a year from our departure. We come back to visit and to do an evaluation. I am interested in how the transition is going for the church and the new preacher.

I like to ask and take notes on answers to two questions about our interim ministry:
   1. What went well?
   2. What improvements would you suggest? I love criticism. Suggestions from previous churches can improve our ministry at future churches.

Gail and I consciously say goodbye to people in the community. I start talking with my barber about our departure date. In smaller communities where we get to know people well, Gail has cooked "goodies" to deliver to people we've known and who have served us well: barber, post office, Y.M.C.A., and individuals in the grocery store in a small town.

Brethren have been gracious. They usually have a going away party for us. I've talked to preachers who rejected such offers because they said it made them feel uncomfortable. I suggest, if that's true with you, be uncomfortable. It's not just about you. Others need a "funeral" to say goodbye.

Solomon stated a good principle when he wrote:
> Better to go to the house of mourning
> Than to go to the house of feasting,
> For that is the end of all men;
> And the living will take it to heart.
> Sorrow is better than laughter,
> For by a sad countenance the heart is made better
> (Ecclesiastes 7:2, 3).

End well to release the church to love their next preacher and his family and to start clean with the next church in your ministry.

Chapter 43
Evaluation:
What Was Helpful? What Can Be Improved?

After an interim church has announced the new preacher and his arrival date, I go into the goodbye and evaluation mode.

I request evaluations as I leave each congregation. I ask for the elders' suggestions. I ask for staff comments to improve staff meetings and my ministry. Special classes end with an evaluation.

The last meeting of the Transition Monitoring Team includes time for evaluation of how to improve the process and saying goodbye.

I distribute and encourage everyone (men, women, children) to fill out and return Review of Jerrie and Gail Barber's Interim Ministry.

Review of Jerrie and Gail Barber's Interim Ministry

Please Rate: ☆ ☆ ☆ ☆ ☆

Comments:

Pros:

Cons:

Name _____

☐ You have permission to use my comments and my name on your web site.

☐ You have permission to use my comments but not my name on your web site.

☐ Please do not use my comments on your web site.

This is helpful in several ways.

- I gain credibility when people tell how our ministry has been helpful.
- I learn ways to improve at the next church. My commitment to each congregation — I'll do the best I know during this time with you. I'd like to do better at the next church. You'll help me by telling me how to improve.
- I post those who give me permission on my website in two places: the right sidebar. I post a new one each Tuesday. I

add to the list of Reviews of Jerrie and Gail's Interim Ministry each week.

- By posting, I build trust. A leader is someone who can hear what people like and what they don't like. An effective leader asks for more. Many people won't tell their real objections first. My reaction at the first criticism determines whether they'll share their main concerns. Jesus said, "And you shall know the truth, and the truth shall make you free" (John 8:32). People who took time to fill out evaluations see both compliments and criticisms posted for everyone to see.

I gain much from people who want to help. I appreciate each one who shares and evaluates.

Observations
- Few people will tell us what they think of us unless we beg them to do it and thank them when they do.
- Unless we know how we're doing, we may spend a lifetime thinking we are more effective or less effective than we are.
- When we learn, we can improve and enjoy.

I use the same process for improving *New Shepherds Orientation* Workshops.

Chapter 44
When You Don't Need an Interim:
Making a Planned Transition Without an Interim

I've written several chapters explaining the importance of having an interim preacher when the previous preacher has been at the congregation a long time (five years or more). We've discussed the necessity of grief, wandering in the wilderness during the time of disorientation. I've written about evaluating strengths needed for the next preacher at this church, the search process, preceded by a self-study, meetings of a Transition Monitoring Team, and other tasks of preparing for the next phase of this congregation.

I want to end this with a final suggestion: you may not need an interim preacher, even after a long ministry.

Suggestions for a Good Transition Without an Intentional Interim

• **Intentionally grow as an eldership and staff.** Every year there should be continuing education for elders, deacons, preachers, and secretaries who will plan classes and learning activities for the entire church. There are so many areas for growth: Bible study, communication, evangelism, counseling, and technology. My forgettery works better than my memory. If I don't grow by learning and experiencing new ideas, I'll drain in knowledge and enthusiasm, become stale, notice things aren't going very well, and start blaming everyone else because the church isn't growing as it should.

• **Start the next transition before your previous preacher has preached his first sermon.** Two things that upset a congregation:

> ▸ A well-loved preacher finding a new place to preach and suddenly announcing it to the congregation.

> ▸ A well-loved preacher suddenly being informed by the elders he is no longer needed and wanted at this church. Observation: even if a preacher is considered unliked and incompetent by some, if he has been at the church more than six months, he will have friends who will be upset by his sudden dismissal.

• **My recommendation to prevent both:**

> ▸ **Before the first sermon, talk about how long the preacher plans to stay and how long the elders want him to stay.** There should be a common understanding before beginning. If a preacher wants to move every three years so he can recycle his sermons and the elders want a long-term ministry, there will be

disappointment. If the preacher sells his house in the previous location, buys a house in this town with the aim of staying many years, and the elders inform him four years and six months after he arrives he needs to start looking for another church because their practice is to change preachers every five years, there will be disappointment.

▸ **Before the first sermon, discuss with the preacher not only how long he'd like to stay but also how he plans to leave, especially if the elders get ready for him to leave before he gets ready.** Many preachers have ruined an otherwise good ministry by throwing a fit on the way out.

▸ **Get the agreements from both the elders and the preacher in writing and review them once a year.** If the preacher plans to stay until retirement, discuss his plans for all aspects of his retirement: finances, his and the elders' expectations after his pulpit time is over, where he plans to live, and how he plans to give space and encouragement for the new preacher. If anyone is reconsidering the initial intent, discuss it.

• **As the time for a change draws closer, continue talking with more details of how to make a helpful transition.** One suggestion I read, was to give the preacher a three-month sabbatical seven years before his retirement for him to rest and plan for his finish in the next seven years to make them the best years of his ministry. That's what we did at Berry's Chapel. We didn't know we were doing it right, but it was the best gift I've ever been given as a preacher. We started talking about three and a half years before I left and I announced my retirement three years before. The elders said, "As far as we know, there's never been a planned transition at Berry's Chapel. We'd like to try it once and see how it works." From my perspective and their continued peaceful good work, it was a good transition.

- **Cultivate honest, open communication.**
  - ▸ **There should be freely flowing verbal and non-verbal communication expressing encouragement and gratitude — both planned and spontaneous.** Prayers, public and private, will often thank God for the elders, preachers, spouses, other leaders, and every member of the congregation. Writing notes of gratitude for specific acts will show and remind everyone of the unity that exists in leadership.

  - ▸ **It will be healthy to have planned, caring, consistent, and creative conflict where disagreement is encouraged and appreciated.** If everyone always agrees with the same person, the rest can be dismissed. A group is deprived of wisdom when most or all are afraid to disagree and express their thoughts and feelings. Without rules and an atmosphere of being able to disagree and question, there will eventually be a major conflict that will not be planned, caring, consistent, and creative. Then you will need an interim.

Three Helpful Books

Two books with good ideas about how to plan for a transition:

1. *Next: Pastoral Succession That Works*, by William Vanderbloemen and Warren Bird

2. *Transition Plan: 7 Secrets Every Leader Needs to Know*, by Bob Russell

One book to give a bad example of how not to do it:

3. *Too Great a Temptation: The Seductive Power of America's Super Church*, by Dr. Joel Gregory

Summary: intentionally go through the discipline of constant growth, practice building good relationships, engage in honest discussions of painful as well as pleasant topics, continue to encourage and care for each other, especially in the leadership team, and plan a good funeral for your relationship before you die (literally or figuratively). Many relationships die years before they end and everyone wonders what went wrong. L. W. White wrote a country song first released in 1971 with the refrain: "there's nothin' cold as ashes after the fire is gone." That's not only true of some marriages but also of too many elder-preacher-church relationships.

With good planning, prayer, and hard work, it can be a good, sad, and happy ending with even better days ahead.

Appendix

Questions to Learn More about Your Family

- What are some of your earliest memories?
- How did you feel "special" in your own family?
- Which parent did you feel closest to?
- What do you see as particular strengths in your family life?
- How did you and your family members deal with conflict?
- Who were you closest to in your family of origin?
- How are you different from others in your family of origin?
- How are you the same?
- What was your life like before I was born? At the time I was born?
- What were some of the most significant turning points in your life?
- Who are the significant people in your life?
- What goals did you establish for yourself in life? How close have you come, would you say, to accomplishing them?

- What goals do you have now?
- Who do you learn most from in your family?
- What are your most satisfying accomplishments?
- What was your biggest challenge as a partner in a marriage/relationship? As a parent?
- How did you deal with it?
- Was religion or faith important to you or your family?
- How did you develop your faith?
- What beliefs are most important to you?
- What was an important religious experience for you?
- What qualities do you appreciate most in your parents? Your siblings?
- What are some of your most important discoveries as a parent?
- How do you make decisions? Who do you talk to about them?
- How do you deal with conflict with (parents, partner, children, etc.)?
- Whose death in the family has affected you the most?

— from *Family Ties that Bind*, by Dr. Ronald W. Richardson, pages 120, 121

Working Agreement

Interim Minister — Transition Consultant Job Description and Contract Between Jerrie W. Barber and Anytown Church of Christ

Function: Interim Preacher and Consultant

Purpose: To serve the congregation as a preacher and consultant, to work with the elders and other leaders in the congregation, to equip the saints for the work of ministry, and the edifying of the body of Christ.

Responsibilities

Pulpit Preaching:
1. Preach at Sunday morning and evening services.
2. Spiritually feed the flock with challenging yet practical applications.
3. Communicate transition plans, ideas, processes, etc.
4. Help us continue our focus on serving Jesus and others.

Teaching:
1. Teach class Sunday morning and Wednesday evening.

2. Lead special studies, such as Learning to Love my Friend(s) for elders and spouses and others if they desire.

3. Facilitate a leadership class, God's Great Servants, for elders, deacons, and those interested in becoming leaders and following leaders better.

Elders:

1. Aid to build relationship and trust between elders and the congregation.

2. Help with communication to congregation, keeping them informed and updated.

3. Assist with formation and administration of a search committee.

4. Serve as a consultant and trainer for the Preacher Search Committee and Transition Monitoring Team.

5. Meet with the elders, at regularly scheduled monthly meetings or at times otherwise requested, to serve as a consultant and resource person.

6. Share thoughts, ideas, suggestions and new possibilities, all with the understanding that the wastebasket exists.

7. Have an open, honest, responsible, respectful relationship with the elders.

8. Provide evaluation of relationship, giving both strong points and those needing improvement.

9. Lead New Shepherds Orientation Workshop for elders, deacons, and wives soon after beginning at Anytown Church of Christ.

Other:

1. Organize and facilitate a self-study to learn who we are, who we would like to be, and what we expect in the next preacher at this church.
2. Be available during day or evening to meet with individuals and groups.
3. If requested, perform weddings and conduct funerals.
4. Interact with many in the congregation, both individually and in groups, to make this time of transition in the church an occasion for individuals and groups to learn about change in their lives and see opportunities for growth.
5. Generally assist with the keeping of set goals and objectives.
6. Be open to suggestions and comments.
7. Any criticism of Jerrie Barber will be directed to Jerrie Barber and it will be welcomed. Jerrie Barber does not accept anonymous criticism.
8. Additional responsibilities and assignments as mutually agreed upon with elders.

Preacher – Church Agreements

1. The salary will be $00,000.00 per year, paid once a month.
2. Jerrie will be allowed one week off each month to hold meetings or workshops or for vacation time.
3. He will have two days off per week to use as he desires.
4. Jerrie will use the preacher's office while he is working at Anytown Church of Christ.
5. Jerrie will do some of his study at home. However, he will be in contact with the office and will be available during regular work days. He will leave contact information on days off as well.
6. The length of our work together will be six to eighteen months. It could be shorter if the elders find a preacher before that time.
7. Either party will give a ninety-day notice for terminating this agreement. From the Sunday a new preacher is announced, Jerrie Barber is to receive ninety days' compensation unless it is less than ninety days to the end of this contract. If it is less than ninety days, he will be paid to the end of this contract. He will either preach or not preach during this time according to the desires of the elders.
8. It is understood that under no circumstances will Jerrie W. Barber consider or be considered as the next full-time preacher for this congregation.

9. Any changes in these agreements will be made only after discussion of all parties involved and would include a signed addendum to the contract.

Elders:

_____

John Doe

_____

James Smith

Preacher:

_____

Jerrie W. Barber

Preacher Chain Letter

Dear Search Committee,

This is a chain letter. The result of a computerized survey indicates that the perfect preacher:

Preaches 15 minutes

Condemns sin; but never offends anyone

Works from 8 am till midnight including janitorial work

Makes $60 per week, wears good clothes, buys good books, drives a good car and gives $50 per week to the poor

Is 28 years old and has been preaching for 30 years

Wonderfully, perfectly handsome

Has a burning desire to work with teenagers but spends all his time with the older folk

Smiles with a straight face because his sense of humor keeps him seriously dedicated to his work.

He makes 15 calls per day on church family, shut-ins, hospitalized, while evangelizing the lost

He is always in his office when needed.

If your preacher does not measure up to this chain letter, send this letter to six other churches who also are tired of their preacher. Bundle up your preacher and send him to the church at the top of the list. In one year you will receive 1,643 preachers. One of them should be perfect.

WARNING: Keep this letter going. One church broke the chain and got their old preacher back in six months.

Phone Screen Interview Questions for Search Committee

Instructions: Each member of the committee should have a copy of these questions. Carefully choose from the following list the questions that your committee feels are pertinent to your church. Check the questions that you would like to ask. The list is not intended to be exhaustive, or to be used in its entirety, or in a particular order, although it could be. Take notes during the interview and rate the candidate on a scale of 1 to 5 for each category. Once the interview is over, transfer your scores to the Interview Summary.

Name of Candidate: _____

Date: _____

Overview
- Goal is to establish common goals, values and expectations with candidates.
- Tactics: Using questions such as those identified below, invite personal stories (e.g., don't ask "what would you do if..." but ask "what have you done when...")

Questions for Search Committee Interviews
Introductory Questions (Break the ice & get general information.)

- Describe your current church, your responsibilities in your current position and results that have been achieved.
- What do you know about our church?
- Can you tell us a little about yourself?
- Why did you choose the schools you attended? How have they shaped your thinking and values?

Bible Scholar Questions (Determine how he sees and uses the Bible.)

- Probing questions on critical issues: describe interpretation of role of women in church/music/baptism etc.

Intrinsic Motivation Questions (Identify sufficient skills/ energy to work toward excellence.)

- When you have been in a leadership role, what have been your biggest disappointments?
- Why did you choose to work in the ministry?
- Which tasks in pulpit ministry bring energy and joy in your life?

Ministry Philosophy Questions (Identify sufficiency of understanding of demands/functions/roles of pulpit minister job.)

- What do you view as the primary (most important) priorities as a minister?
- What issues, concerns and attitudes are dominant in your current church?
- In what ways have you given leadership to the church in evangelism and church growth?
- Why do you believe that the context for this church is the right setting for you and your family to minister?
- Who is your ministry role model?
- Name a few churches that you think follow your philosophy of ministry. Why?
- What does your ideal church look like?
- Tell us about one thing that has happened at your current job that is a good example of your philosophy.

Relationship Questions (Determine how he will interact with others, including minister peers.)

- What advantages and complexities do you see from working with a large ministerial staff like ours?
- Where do you see youth ministry fitting into the total life of our congregation?
- What are your strengths as far as people skills are concerned?
- Tell us about your leadership style.
- Have you ever been in a situation with a strong-willed individual whose ideas were not compatible with your

vision? How did you resolve those differences? Would you handle it differently now?

Job Performance Questions

- What have you learned at your current church that will help you be an even better leader here?
- Why are you leaving your present job?
- What did you like/dislike about your current job?
- What would your current employer say about you?
- Please briefly explain the circumstances surrounding your ministry changes in the past. What are the main factors for why you are open to a possible ministry change to our church in the future?
- Describe your experience in working with a budget.

Education Questions

- Have you had any other special training?
- Have you attended any relevant conferences or seminars?
- Cite some of your publications and speaking engagements.
- What was the most valuable aspect of your college education?
- What are a few books that you have read in the past few years which are related to your field?

Any additional notes or comments:

Pulpit Minister Interview Questions

Applicant: _____

Date: _____

Tell us about yourself and your family (not your education or work experience, but about you the person.)

Briefly discuss your education and work experience, how you came to be employed at each place, what you accomplished, and why you left each place.

Please tell us about your conversion.

What are your gifts and how have you used them?

Discuss your involvement in the community where you presently serve.

Tell us about your mentors and name some ministers in the church that you highly respect and explain why.

What are some things you do to ensure you are growing as a person, minister, and leader?

How would you describe your leadership style?

What are your specific beliefs regarding:
Baptism.
Divorce and remarriage.
Role of women in the church.

Give an overview of a sermon series you have preached and the most difficult sermon you have preached.

How would you react if a member came up to you publicly after a sermon and harshly criticized you about its Biblical accuracy or about a life application point you had made?

When was the last time you were really upset about something that occurred at church?

Which version of the Bible do you prefer using and why?

How do you feel about a congregation having a vision and can you share visions of previous congregations?

What do you recall from having studied the Member Survey? What excites you and concerns you the most about the survey?

The congregation, in the survey, favors developing deeper spiritual relationships, sharing the gospel with the unsaved, meaningful worship experience, and helping members discover their own gifts for ministry and service. What do you see as the preacher/minister role in accomplishing these things?

What do we, as a congregation, need to do to fulfill our Christian ministry – individually and in a congregational setting?

In a congregation as large as this one, there are a diversity of beliefs, backgrounds, and thoughts on how we function as a group of Christians. How would your sermons satisfy these wide-based needs?

What do you think constitutes a meaningful worship service, and what is the preacher's role in this (or how does the sermon contribute)?

How do you balance your sermons between "first principles" to reach the unsaved and "Christian growth" principles to encourage members with a range of growth stages?

How do you approach doctrinal subjects from a "truth standpoint" without it coming across as just "Church of Christ" doctrine or heritage view?

Do you feel that "small group" meetings in addition to corporate worship and Bible study times have a role in

Christian growth? How can they be accomplished without being viewed as dividing the congregation?

How important do you feel communications are to congregational unity? How does the preacher/minister fill a role in encouraging better communications?

In addition to the sermons and lessons he would present, how important is the conduct of the minister's daily life as an example to the congregation?

How much of a role do you feel a preacher should have in "church management" in a congregation the size of this congregation, versus the role as preacher, teacher, evangelizer, and encourager?

What is your policy/practice regarding doing funerals?

Describe your current schedule for a typical week and how much of this time do you think is appropriate to spend in the church office?

How often do you visit hospitals nursing homes, and shut-ins?

How would you describe your working relationship with other ministers and staff members in your previous and current workplaces?

Have you received regular performance appraisals at your present or past congregations? If so, please summarize those for us. To follow up, what would your current shepherds tell us about your strengths and weaknesses?

What is the worst thing we could find out about you when doing a detailed background check? Have you ever filed bankruptcy, defaulted on a loan, been taken to court or taken someone else to court?

If evaluating your own spiritual and personal areas of growth, what would you change about yourself and what could we do to help you?

What is your understanding of the role of elders?

Describe what you consider to be an ideal working relationship between the pulpit minister and the elders.

Please discuss any spiritual understanding you have of a subject which might cause us or our leadership any concern.

What do you consider some of the major problems facing the church today? Which of these problems upset you the most, and what do you do to deal with them effectively?

Do you perform marriage ceremonies for anyone who asks you?

What is your philosophy as it relates to counseling?

Describe some new ideas your congregation has implemented that have made a positive difference and what was your role?

How have you dealt with the young professional age group, and what are your ideas to encourage and support this involved group at this church?

Is there a favorite age or gender group you prefer to teach?

Please share your ideas on helping to develop leadership skills.

How many Sundays were you out of the pulpit last year, and what are your scheduled engagements for this year?

How would you describe your congregation's growth in the past five years?

How important are Sunday night services and how do you prepare for the service compared to Sunday morning?

How do you ensure you maintain healthy balance between church and family life, and does this affect you being available to the congregation after hours?

How involved are your wife and children in church activities?

What are some of the goals you have set for yourself this year and what do you hope to be doing five (5) and ten (10) years from now?

What would you be doing if you were not in ministry?

If you are selected to come to this congregation, what can we do to make the transition a smooth and positive experience for your family?

Why should we hire you to be our next pulpit minister?

What questions do you have?

Would you like to make any closing statements?

Interviewer Comments:

Pulpit Minister Interview Summary

A printable PDF is available online at http://jerriebarber.com/wp-content/uploads/2016/01/03-Interview-Summary-Chart-1.pdf

Interview Summary (rate on a scale of 1-5)	Excellent 5 Points	Very Good 4 Points	Good 3 Points	Fair 2 Points	Poor 1 Point
Canadidate's name:					
Date of interview:					
How would you rate the *Overview* conversation?					
How would you rate the *Introductory* conversation?					
How would you rate the *Bible Scholar* questions?					
How would you rate the *Intrinsic Motivation* questions?					
How would you rate the *Ministry Philosophy* questions?					
How would you rate the *Relationship* questions?					
How would you rate the *Job Performance* questions?					
How would you rate the *Educational* questions?					
How would you rate the candidate's *Passon for Teaching* ?					
How would you rate the candidate's *Interest in a challenge* ?					
How would you rate his *Attitude* ?					
Total score of each category					
Total score all catagories					
A = 45 to 55 total points					
B = 35 to 44 total points					
C = 25 to 34 total points					

Letter to Applicant

Hometown Church

1122 Street

Town, State 00000

Date

[Insert Name]

[Insert Address Line 1]

[Insert Address Line 2]

Re: Hometown Church Pulpit Minister Position

Dear [Insert Name]:

On Behalf of the Search and Interview committee, I want to thank you for your interest in being considered for the Pulpit Minister position at the Hometown Church. We will be reviewing your résumé and qualifications to determine if there is a genuine interest in speaking with you further. If so, a member of the Search Committee will be in touch with you via telephone to set up a phone interview. We understand the importance of confidentiality and assure you your résumé will remain confidential.

We are excited about the opportunities we have ahead of us at the Hometown Church and we trust that God has great plans for you as well. Thank you again for your interest.

With Highest Regard,

[Signature of Committee Member]

[Insert Name of Committee Member]
On Behalf of the Search Committee

Letter of Regret

Hometown Church

1122 Street

Town, State 00000

Date

[Insert Name]

[Insert Address Line 1]

[Insert Address Line 2]

Re: Hometown Church Pulpit Minister Position

Dear [Insert Name]:

On behalf of the Search and Interview committee, I want to thank you for your interest in the Pulpit Minister position at the Hometown Church. Unfortunately, after carefully reviewing your qualifications and conducting a phone interview with you we have determined that your résumé and qualifications are not compatible with the criteria set forth by our eldership for the pulpit position of the Hometown Church. We understand the importance of confidentiality and assure you your time spent with us will remain confidential.

We are excited about the opportunities we have ahead of us at the Hometown Church and we trust that God has great plans for you as well. Thank you again for your interest.

With Highest Regard,

[Signature of Committee Member]

[Insert Name of Committee Member]
On Behalf of the Search Committee

Preachers Questions for Elders:
Dale Jenkins

A couple of quick disclaimers:

I love elders! I've been blessed to work with twenty-five to fifty elders and by and large they are the very best men I've ever known!

While I don't purport to be an expert I'll start a list and let your comments add to it.

You want to watch how the elders interact with each other. Do they seem to get along? Is there a comfort or a tension when they are together? Are they real or artificial? Do they treat each other as peers or does one dominate? You might even ask that last as a question and WATCH their reaction. Now, you may or may not like what you learn; and that may not be a reason to go or not, BUT at least you know what you are getting and have to work with or toward.

A lot of guys get all antsy about matters of opinion and there is some reason to know where they are on some issues. BUT, I'd suggest that may be even more important is how they handle their positions on those issues. If you talk long enough and/or work together long enough you WILL find areas where you do not agree. So, do they think about people more than the position? Are they sensitive and caring in dealing with "hard" positions or do they just plow forward? Is every "position" written in stone or are they willing to discuss? Do they have a know-it-all attitude or are they still learning? How do they treat people who differ from themselves? What do they say about those people in private?

How do they deal with money? Are they a bunch of tightwads who wouldn't let go of a dollar for a soul or are they willing to spend to help for LOCAL outreach? Do they think a preacher should make "x" number of dollars or will you get cost of living raises (if you don't get at least that, you are in reality making LESS each year)? My advice is that you ask them for a cost of living raise each year in advance. I always ask that elders at least discuss what I am paid each year–they may or may not give me a raise–but I don't want five years to go by and they have not even thought of it.

Can they be wrong and admit it? Many elderships can't admit they are human–of course they will say they are–but they would never say–"We blew it." Some elderships are like the Fonz–"I was wrrrrnn...rrrrggg...wrrr". Ask them when was the last time they made a mistake and what it was. Did they own it?

How do they appoint new elders? There are many ways to go about this process. Some elders think the way they do it is set in stone. Some elders treat themselves like a "self-perpetuating board." I do believe that elders can biblically appoint additional elders in a congregation–if they were selected to lead the church then that would be a form of leadership. But in our day it seems wise to involve the members in the process. I've seen elders who refuse to appoint others as elders because they "think differently" than we do. I understand, that but it's a dangerous route.

Do they love the lost or just enjoy diverting attention? Often elderships seem to enjoy chasing rabbits and spinning their wheels on issues and problems rather than dealing with souls. Do they take time to pray for the lost and the fallen? Do they dismiss their responsibility or are they active in reaching the lost in the community ("beginning at Jerusalem")?

Do they listen to the congregation? Do they think all practical wisdom resides within the three or six of them or are they wise enough to ask for input and help from the congregation? I've known churches with faithful, professional decorators in the body who determined colors and styles without any input. That sort of thing could be said of a myriad of issues. It is hard to keep the congregation together if they believe the elders do not respect them.

Preachers Questions for Elders:
Bryan McAlister

Thanks for the opportunity to share. There are dozens of questions one should ask when entering this kind of relationship. There are two that I have relied on to "gauge" an eldership's demeanor in the early days of the relationship.

> What would it take to sever our relationship? (Beyond the obvious moral and doctrinal implications, what do they not want to see in me, so I can avoid doing that?)

> What is the eldership's policy/position on continuing education? (This was significant to me in order to see how the elders felt about my growth and learning)

There is a third question, once the "screening" questions have been asked of me. I'm not sure if it is a question or a statement intended to convey a deeper sentiment.

> Now that you have asked about my beliefs and faith, I'm curious when you will ask if I pray and how often? Or if I treat my wife and children with love and respect?

I recognize that such questions could be perceived as pompous, but that was not my intention. The third is more of a revelation for the minister to the elders that shows this role transcends the presence in a pulpit or the occupation of an office space.

Preachers Questions for Elders
Jeremy Houck

How would you describe your church? Does the church describe itself by its past or by its vision? Do core values look inward or outward?

Why was the church started? If a split that happened over 100 years ago started this congregation, there still may be some baggage.

What is the church's Purpose? Does it have a well-defined mission and strategy or do they go with the flow?

What is your unique role in this community? What sets this church apart? Who is the target audience? What ministry do they offer that no one else offers?

How would a neighbor around this building portray this congregation? This tells you a lot about a church's outreach.

What's this church's theology? Does the church commit that Jesus is the head?

How would you describe the atmosphere of: Worship; Small Groups; Business Meetings; Family Meetings; Special Events? Do they all agree on these?

What are three areas that you feel need to be changed in this church? What are three areas that you feel need to stay the same? This will tell you the strengths and weaknesses of this congregation.

How many strong ministries does this church have? The more ministries, the more involved the membership is.

What new ministries have been started in the last five years? If none, you may encounter "we've never done it that way before."

If you knew you couldn't fail, what would your dreams be for this church? If they do not have dreams then neither will the congregation.

What are the statistics for worship over the past five years? This gives you clues to tension and splits.

Do you have a plan for growth? Are they willing to pay the price for growth?

What is the single biggest obstacle for growth in this church? If they all agree, you know where to start; if they disagree you need to work on aligning perceptions.

What role do you feel ministers should play in the development of a strong, growing, congregation? Vision will vary here but it makes them think.

When did your last new members join? If the last family placed membership three years ago, you need to look at stale ministries.

Is there any conflict in the church now? Conflict should not surprise you but it will allow the committee to be honest.

What issues have regularly caused friction in this church? Are these real issues or symptoms?

Why do you think I will help this church? The answers will shed light on expectations.

What were the strengths and weaknesses of the past preacher? Do they dwell on the negative or push the positive? This also gives more expectations.

How long have previous ministers worked with this congregation? This pattern will usually follow. If the old minister retired then are you the interim?

How does this church view its staff? Are they professionals or are they hired help?

To whom do I answer and who will answer to me? This shows the hierarchy. You should answer directly to the elders.

Has the interim period been healing? Interims are very helpful. Was it outside help or another minister on staff?

What is the role of the preacher? Is he the office manager, mentor, or does he run the show?

Will I have the freedom to shape and form my own ministry team? Or are you expected to work with the old team and their old ties and baggage?

What is expected of my family? Is your wife expected at every event? Does she have to lead a ministry? Does your family have to answer to the elders or are you allowed to be the head of the home?

Notes on Church Visit During Tryout

When I was "trying out" my wife, my daughter, and I filled our "Shoney's Mystery Shopper Reports" on each congregation we visited. See chapter on: Suggestions for the Preacher Search — Suggestions from Observation and Experience About Looking for a Preacher (Chapter 35)

Here are two of the combined reports:

Church # 1

Elders
Elder 1 Phone #
Elder 2
Elder 3 Phone #

OBSERVATIONS 01/01/0000
- John Doe called, had heard I needed $00, 000 (incorrect high amount) per year; told to forget it by a deacon
- received motel confirmation in mail 01/01/0000
- natural beauty, mountains
- good reception from congregation
- plans to build new wing with offices
- housing costs probably very reasonable

- prompt response from secretary with two tapes of former preacher, encouraging letter also adding name to bulletin list
- bulletin printing quality, good
- note from John and Mary Smith, Bob and Sue Jones
- note from Tom and Nancy Johnson
- note from Don and Jane Thomas

- indicated lack of written job description and contract and communicated no plans to have one
- morning and evening worship on radio with time limitations - lack of focus on work of church; tape sermons "to prove what preacher said"
- elders had fixed agenda ready to end interview after discussing their subjects
- daily radio program with a preference for live broadcasts
- controversy over Masonic Lodge issue
- building poorly organized
- few young people

Church # 2

Elders
Elder 1 Phone
Elder 2 Phone
Elder 3 Phone

Associate Preacher Phone
Wife
Children

John and Mary Doe, supper at Peddlers

Tom Jones
member of search committee
friends of Henry and Linda Smith, supper at Peddlers –
member of search committee

OBSERVATiONS
Date

- Calls from Elder 1
- calls from Associate Preacher, directions, time, change in time circumstances, etc.
- good attitude toward and presentation of congregation and work by Associate Preacher

- nice building, circular auditorium, PA system, pulpit area spacious office, book cases
- definiteness in plan of search
- search committee meets each Wednesday night committee from 20's, 30's, 40's evaluation from congregation
- expenses + $00.00 per presentation + $00.00 (they had a plan)
- references had been checked
- special arrangements for Wednesday night
- good attendance
- sister congregation taught Bible classes in order that teachers might hear try-out lesson
- natural beauty in area - hills, mountains
- each elder talked at ease, felt comfortable in process
- Elder 3 and another family visited my home congregation, date
- Elder 1 had listened to tapes of meeting where I preached recently
- congregation—good attention during preaching, expressive and appreciative after services, feel of family unity
- didn't seem overly concerned, didn't mention salary, benefits, etc.
- expressed and demonstrated lack of time pressure to secure preacher
- prompt response from Associate Preacher, sending tapes and sermon outline as requested

- call, date, from Elder 1 and Elder 3, gave results of Sunday survey
- call, date, from Elder 1 and Elder 2; confirmed receipt of letter and continued interest indicated that they had no plans to have another preacher in until they heard from me
- call, date, to set up time for next visit
- flexibility in preacher's job description
- communicated willingness to have written contract and job description
- 20 minutes from airport

- lack of eye contact
- cost of housing
- deacons with no specific areas of work - honorary deacons
- history of preachers with short tenure
- secretary?
- very concerned about "legal" issues — whether one must confess publicly for forsaking the assembly, not tuned to "heart" issues
- who will be team leader?
- assigned sermon topics for try-out Sunday

Preacher Interview

Congregation: _____

Name: _____

Date: _____

1. What has been the growth history of this congregation?

2. What opportunities do you see for future growth?

3. What kind of preacher is needed for this congregation at this time?

4. What is the reputation in the community?

5. What is the reputation and relationship with area congregations?

6. What is expected of the preacher?

7. Who are the elders?

Name	Occupation	Service
_____	_____	_____
_____	_____	_____

_____

_____

8. How do the elders function? (administrators, shepherds, bosses, deacons, workers, etc.)

9. How do the elders handle conflict?
   a. How do they deal with anger?
   b. How do they keep commitments?
   c. How do they apologize?

10. How do the elders express tenderness, gratitude, concern?
    a. How do they honor each other?
    b. How do they honor others?
    c. How do they practice hospitality?
       (1) How often have they been in your home?
       (2) How often have you been invited into their homes?

11. What is the elder-preacher relationship?
    a. Meetings?
    b. Exchange and acceptance of ideas?
    c. Outside "church"?

12. What kind of vision (sense of purpose) do the elders have?

13. How do the elders grow?

14. What is the staff relationship?

    a. How often do you have staff meetings?

    b. What do you do in staff meetings?

15. What is a vital need of this congregation?

16. What are the strengths of this congregation?

17. What are the weaknesses of this congregation?

18. How has your family been received and treated?

    a. What is expected and permitted in regard to your wife?

    b. Children?

19. Matthew 7:12 - If I were in your place and you were in mine, what would you want me to tell you?

Staff Interview

Congregation: _____

Name: _____

Date: _____

1. What has been the growth history of this congregation?

2. What opportunities do you see for future growth?

3. What kind of preacher is needed for this congregation at this time?

4. What is the reputation in the community?

5. What is the reputation and relationship with area congregations?

6. What is expected of the preacher?

7. What is the staff relationship?
    a. How often do you have staff meetings?
    b. What do you do in staff meetings?

8. What is a vital need of this congregation?

9. What are some strengths of this congregation?

10. What are some weaknesses of this congregation?

11. How has your family been received and treated?
    a. What is expected and permitted in regard to your wife (husband)?
    b. Children?

12. Matthew 7:12 - If I were in your place and you were in mine, what would you want me to tell you?

Thank You

In addition to the two final proof-readers, several have considered this book and have given valuable suggestions and encouragement. They are not responsible for the final product. I take all responsibility and blame for that.

They have been encouraging in my ministry and in the preparation of this book:

Tony Duncan

Nathan Foster

Carlus Gupton

Willie Hamblen

Jeremy Houck

Dale Jenkins

Roger Leonard

Bryan McAlister

Dean Miller

John Parker

Ron Sandefur

Andy Walker

Randy Willingham

Ken Wilson

The elders of the Berry's Chapel Church of Christ in Franklin, Tennessee have been helpful to Gail and me since we started working with them in June 1993. I told them when I came I wanted to do interim ministry before I was too old. They continually helped and encouraged this work by word and paying for my training with the Interim Ministry Network. This was my last and longest full-time work.

Thank you:

Dennis Crowder

Taft Davis

Ron Gambill

Jim Hestle

Jim Hightower

Joe King

Dennis Makings

Mike Norwood

Charlie Shipley

John Smith

Bill Thornton

Tom Vaughn

Channing Workman

About the Author

Jerrie Barber has been preaching since June 18, 1961. He and his wife, Gail, have been doing interim ministry since May 2007. They married August 18, 1964, have two married children, six grandchildren, and three great-grandchildren.

jerrie@barberclippings.com

newshepherdsorientation.com
jerriebarber.com

@JerrieWBarber

www.ingramcontent.com/pod-product-compliance
Lightning Source LLC
LaVergne TN
LVHW041314080426
835513LV00008B/456